Understanding God's Purpose for the Anointing
by
Creflo A. Dollar Jr.

If you would like more information about this ministry, or are interested in becoming a partner, please write:
WORLD CHANGERS MINISTRIES
Post Office Box 490124
College Park, Georgia 30349

Editorial and Creative services provided by:
Vision Communications
169 E. 32nd
Edmond, OK 73013
(405) 348-7995

Understanding God's Purpose for the Anointing
ISBN: 0-9634781-0-9

Table of Contents

Dedication

I would like to dedicate this book to my spiritual father and mother, Kenneth and Gloria Copeland. I thank God for you both. You will never know the impact that you have had on my life and ministry. Thank you for everything.

Preface

In early 1991 I found myself at a spiritual crossroad, not having any idea what God wanted to do next in my life and ministry. I knew in my spirit that the decade of the '90's was going to be different. I knew that if I (or any other believer) was going to survive, much less thrive, I would have to know what God was saying. I was convinced that I could no longer accomplish things by my own plans, decisions and good ideas. With this in mind, I went before the Lord to seek direction.

As I prayed, He spoke to me saying, "Son, it is time for an overhaul!"

"An *overhaul?*" I thought. "What does He mean by that?"

Then I realized that, naturally speaking, when an engine gets an overhaul, it is completely rebuilt and reassembled so that it can function and operate as though it were brand new. I knew that was exactly what I needed!

I realized I needed to be rebuilt and reconstructed in the Word so that I could make it through the demanding days to come. I knew it was time to slip away from the daily pressures and duties of pastoring a large and growing church, and go away to seek the Lord. My wife began to sense this need as well. So, she arranged for us to go to a remote island in the Carolinas. We left determined not to return until we had the Word of the Lord for the rest of the journey. We *had* to have God's instructions.

While at the island, we did nothing but fast, pray and seek God. One morning, after a time in the Word, I decided to pray in the Spirit until something broke loose and was released inside of me. As I prayed, a powerful force suddenly began to swell up on the inside of my spirit. My entire body began to shake and I could sense the manifested presence of God surrounding me. Then, the Spirit of the Lord spoke to my spirit, saying:

In order for you to get the rest of the way. . . in order for the entire body of Christ to get the rest of the way, everyone must be clothed with my ability, my virtue, my power and my anointing. There are some yokes that you will encounter that cannot be broken with your own natural abilities, but it is going to require Me and My abilities to break them. YOU MUST HAVE MY ANOINTING!

That was that. It was all I needed to know. I had the Word of the Lord.

You see, child of God, you are going to encounter things in these last days that will confound all of the education and natural ability in the world. However, with the anointing of God, you will be able to handle these challenges masterfully and victoriously. You cannot do it alone. You must say "good-bye" to the old Lone Ranger mentality, and say "hello" to the anointing of God. *You must have God's anointing.* Without it, you will not succeed.

In the following pages you will discover what the anointing is, how it operates and how you can make it a permanent part of your daily life. Once that happens, no challenge will face you that you cannot overcome, no weapon the devil may send against you can catch you by surprise or do you harm and no circumstance can steal your joy and peace.

It is with this in mind that I present to you what I believe is an absolutely essential message for everyone in the Body of Christ to know and understand—"God's Purpose for the Anointing."

Chapter 1
From Humility to the Anointing

"The fear of the Lord is the instruction of wisdom; and before honour is humility." **Proverbs 15:33**

The Anointing. That term is thrown around a lot in Christian circles today. "He's a very anointed speaker...She has a real anointing for that...The anointing breaks the yoke, you know." You can hear such comments on any given Sunday in any charismatic or Pentecostal church in America.

But what is *The Anointing?*

In the course of this study you'll find out. What's more, you'll learn how you can qualify for and operate in the anointing.

Qualify? Yes! You see, only one type of person is truly able to understand the nature of the anointing and walk in it—and that person is one who has come to the point of genuine humility.

Notice I said *genuine* humility. Most people don't even know what that is. They don't recognize it when they see it because they judge by the wrong criteria. Thus, many of the people we have called humble are actually prideful and vice versa.

What is Humility?

According to the world's standards, a humble man walks around with his head down, his shoulders slouched and doesn't say much. But the world is mistaken. A quiet person is not necessarily a humble person. One can be silent and yet rebellious; quiet and yet selfish.

ne token, a man who walks confidently and _ws who he is, is not necessarily arrogant. *Confidence is not pride.* Consider the confident servant waiting to boldly carry out his master's command. He is confident, yet at the same time, he is yielding to the authority of another.

What, then, is true humility? Let's look at what the Word has to say about it.

Better it is to be of an humble spirit with the lowly, than to divide the spoil with the proud. (Proverbs 16:19)

A man's pride shall bring him low: but honour shall uphold the humble in spirit. (Proverbs 29:23)

When pride cometh, then cometh shame: but with the lowly is wisdom. (Proverbs 11:2)

The Bible says humility is "lowliness" or the act of being lowly. According to these verses, the lowly have wisdom and it's better to have a humble spirit than a spirit of pride.

In a very basic sense, to be humble means to be submissive. It means to take your authority, power and independence and yield them to another. It implies becoming totally obedient to a higher authority. To step down, in order to look up.

Child of God, when you are humble in the sight of God, you place yourself in a lowly position under His mighty hand. You are under His authority and power. You refuse to move until you find out *where* **He** wants you to go, *when* **He** wants you to go and *what* **He** wants you to do when you get there.

A humble man has no plans, programs or ideas of his own. He simply adopts *with all his heart* the plans, programs and ideas of the one to whom he is submitted. No longer independent, he becomes interdependent with the authority over him.

Pride is totally opposite in nature.

A prideful man has a conceited belief in his superiority over others. He exalts his plans, programs and ways of doing things above God's. When you are prideful, you do what **you** want, the way **you** want to do it and when **you** want it done. You live as if you are independent of God's hand and authority.

If you live this way, you will ultimately be brought low. You cannot stand for very long without God's hedge around you. Pride invariably leads to a fall.

"I Know Not!"

What does all this have to do with the anointing? Plenty. Before God ever showed me anything about the anointing, I had to come to the point of true humility. I had to realize that *my* power and *my* ways of doing things were no longer sufficient to accomplish all that God had called me to do.

The same will be true for you. You will have to adopt God's way of doing things before you can enjoy the success the anointing brings. You will have to humble yourself before God can exalt you.

The Bible is full of accounts of men who did exactly that. Take Solomon, for example. In I Kings 3, we see him as a newly crowned king. He had just received a divine visitation during which God told him that He would give him anything he would ask. It was an easy time for Solomon to step into pride, wouldn't you say? But he didn't. He simply prayed:

And now, O Lord my God, thou hast made thy servant king instead of David my father: and I am but a *little child:* I know not how to go out or come in.

And thy servant is in the midst of thy people which thou hast chosen, a great people, that cannot be numbered nor counted for multitude.

Give therefore thy servant an understanding heart to judge thy people, that I may discern between good and bad: for who is able to judge this thy so great a people? (I Kings 3:7-9)

Common sense tells us that when Solomon said, "I am but a little child, I know not how to go out or come in," he was not referring to his age or education. He was a grown man, educated in the household of a king! What he was saying was that he felt inadequate to judge such a great country and that he wanted to receive God's instruction, just as a child does from his parent.

Solomon realized that even with his education and ability he could not succeed apart from God. He made a decision not to act out of his own limited knowledge and resources, but rather to seek God's plans. He called upon God to supernaturally supply what he did not possess naturally, thereby tapping into God's limitless resources and power.

How did God respond to his humble posture? We find out in **I Kings 3:12-14**:

Behold, I have done according to thy words: lo, I have given thee a wise and an understanding heart; so that there was none like thee before thee, neither after thee shall any arise like unto thee.

And I have also given thee that which thou hast not asked, both riches, and honour: so that there shall not be any among the kings like unto thee all thy days.

And if thou wilt walk in my ways, to keep my statutes and my commandments, as thy father David did walk, then I will lengthen thy days.

The Child's Key to Greatness

Compare Solomon's request to Jesus' words in **Matthew 18:3-4.**

Verily I say unto you, Except ye be converted, and become as little children, ye shall not enter into the kingdom of heaven. Whosoever therefore shall humble himself as this little child, the same is greatest in the kingdom of heaven.

In this context, the *kingdom of heaven* refers to the abundant life of righteousness, peace and joy in the Holy Spirit that is ours as joint heirs with Jesus Christ (Romans 14:17). Jesus says we enter into that great, abundant life by humbling ourselves as little children. His words confirm what Solomon demonstrated: *child-like humility ultimately leads to greatness.*

All of us begin our Christian lives with that kind of humility. Unfortunately, we lose it as time goes by. You see it happen in the natural realm to most families.

For example, when children are born into the world, they don't have any of their own plans, abilities or ideas. They must rely completely on the plans and abilities of their parents. But little by little, they begin to develop their own opinions. Gradually, instead of simply learning from their parents, they begin to argue or rebel against them. Where there once was harmony, divisions between the parent and child begin to surface. Once this happens, they can no longer walk together (Amos 3:3).

Sadly, that is precisely what happens to most of us in our relationship to our Heavenly Father.

When we are first born-again, we cannot move without the direction and help of the Holy Spirit. However, after we have been saved for a while and have acquired some knowledge, we start thinking we know how to handle ourselves. We say things like "I've done this before," or "I know how that works." Instead of seeking God's instruction and help the way we used to, we begin to do things our own way. We get proud, independent of God's authority.

How does God respond to that pride? The Bible says, **"God resisteth the proud, but giveth grace unto the humble" (James 4:6).** That should not surprise you. You are the same way with your children. When your child rebels against you and decides to do things his own way, you have a set response. When he decides, "Hey, I'm not going to empty the trash can. I'm not going to cut the grass anymore. I'm going to live life on my terms," your grace stops. You say, "Out, buddy! I resist you!" However, as long as your child is submitted to your authority, you give him grace. He can make all kinds of mistakes, but you still feed, care for and help him every way you can because he is in a submissive position.

Most Christians would deny they have ever lifted themselves up in pride that way against God. But let me ask you; How many Christians are there who say, "Well, I know the Bible teaches tithing, but I just can't afford to tithe right now" or "I know I need to forgive them, but you just don't understand what they have done to me"? Such statements are nothing but pride and rebellion, exalting your own thoughts and feelings above God's Word.

If you have done that in any area of your life, you must humble yourself like a child and get back in the place of God's grace. Come to God and say, "Lord, I submit to you. Show me where to go." If you will do that, He will be faithful to you. If you start going the wrong way, He will do whatever it takes to turn you around. You will walk in blessings and victory you do not deserve. You will walk in grace because of your humility!

From Favor to Failure...And Back Again

Child of God, far too many people have lost all sense of victory in their work, ministry, home life and school work simply because they have expelled God and His ideas from their lives. In so doing, they've fallen from favor to failure.

Let me show you what I mean. Suppose there is a man who wants to be a pastor, but God has called him to be a praise and worship leader. That man can pray, fast, study and work as hard as he wants at being a pastor, but he will never know true success.

Why? Because he has put aside God's plan and design for his life, taken up his own and, subsequently, gone from humility to pride. In the process, he's traded guaranteed victory in the anointing of God for guaranteed failure in his own power.

Satan himself is the earliest scriptural example of someone who made that terrible trade. He was the anointed cherub, highly favored by God, yet in Isaiah 14:12-15, we see that because he said "I will" rather than "Thy will," he was brought down to the pit of hell.

Pride always leads to disaster. If you doubt it, take a look at what happened to King Nebuchadnezzar. His life bore out the truth of **Proverbs 18:12: "Before destruction the heart of man is haughty, and before honour is humility."**

In **Daniel 4:30,** we find him congratulating himself on his own greatness. **"Is not this great Babylon, that I have built for the house of the kingdom by the might of my power, and for the honour of my majesty?"** he says. But his self-adulation doesn't last long. For, as verses 31-37 tell us:

While the word was in the kings mouth, there fell a voice from heaven, saying, O king Nebuchadnezzar, to thee it is spoken; The kingdom is departed

from thee. And they shall drive thee from men, and thy dwelling shall be with the beasts of the field: they shall make thee to eat grass as oxen, and seven times shall pass over thee, until thou know that the Most High ruleth in the kingdom of men, and giveth it to whomsoever he will.

The same hour was the thing fulfilled upon Nebuchadnezzar: and he was driven from men, and did eat grass as oxen, and his body was wet with the dew of heaven, till his hairs were grown like eagles' feathers, and his nails like birds claws.

And at the end of the days I Nebuchadnezzar lifted up mine eyes unto heaven, and mine understanding returned unto me, and I blessed the Most High, and I praised and honoured him that liveth forever, whose dominion is an everlasting dominion, and his kingdom is from generation to generation: And all the inhabitants of the earth are reputed as nothing: and he doeth according to his will in the army of heaven, and among the inhabitants of the earth: and none can stay his hand or say unto him, What doest thou? At the same time my reason returned unto me; and for the glory of my kingdom, mine honour and brightness returned unto me; and my counsellors and my lords sought unto me; and I was established in my kingdom, and excellent majesty was added unto me.

Now I Nebuchadnezzar praise and extol and honour the King of heaven, all whose works are truth, and his ways judgment: and those that walk in pride he is able to abase.

This is a perfect study in the process of pride. In this case, it starts out with tragedy, but, glory to God, it ends in restoration and victory.

In the beginning, we see the pride of this great king evidenced by his heavy use of the words "I" and "my". Then, we see God step in and speak the word of his destruction.

Keep in mind, God will not forcibly humble you, but he can and will use circumstances and situations to influence you. He will not put you down, but He will allow you to trip on your own pride and fall flat on your face. That's exactly what happened to king Nebuchadnezzar; *His downfall wasn't God's fault*, it came as the direct result of his own arrogance.

After he had been brought low, the only thing left for him to do was look up in humility. At the moment he looked up everything was restored to him.

That's what God wants more than anything. If He can somehow get us to look up in humility, He can bless us!

James 4:10 says, **"Humble yourselves in the sight of the Lord, and He shall lift you up."** That means that if you'll get involved with God's plans, they will take you upward to great things.

You may only be making $5.00 an hour right now, but if you'll humble yourself and submit to God's plan of tithing and offering, you will not be making $5.00 an hour for long. God will instantly start you in the process of upward motion. He will immediately give you the power to succeed—and that power is in the anointing.

Get Dressed!

First Peter 5:6 says, **"Humble yourselves therefore under the mighty hand of God, that he may exalt you in due time."** **First Kings 18:46** says that Elijah outran the king's chariots because **"the hand of the Lord was upon him."** Put those two scriptures together, and they prove what I have been saying throughout this chapter: The place of humility is the place of God's power.

It is there, beneath the hand of God, that you have access to supernatural anointing and abilities. It is there where you can throw off the limits of man and operate by the limitless power and might of the Spirit of the living God.

So stop resisting and get humble! As **I Peter 5:5** says, **"...Be subject one to another, and be clothed with humility: for God resisteth the proud, and giveth grace to the humble."**

I like that phrase, "be clothed with humility," because it so accurately depicts our necessary attitude as Christians. We must be clothed with humility in order to walk with God (Micah 6:8). Have you ever seen a mother try to dress her three or four-year old child who has no intention of wearing the clothes she has selected for him? He will fight and squirm against her every effort. By the time she has gotten his arm in one sleeve, he has wiggled free of the other.

It's an exhausting and fruitless endeavor. Yet, most believers behave exactly the same way when it comes to the Anointing! While God is trying to dress them with His power and anointing, they are so busy squirming around, trying to pursue their own plans and ideas, that He can't do a thing with them.

Don't be like that! Comply with and submit to the dressing of the Holy Ghost. Allow those He has placed in authority over you to teach you. Quit arguing with the Bible, and just obey it. Help the Holy Spirit clothe you in the anointing by clothing yourself first with the undergarments of humility.

Humility is the key to all of God's power. It is the foundation and prerequisite for all blessing and honor. Oh, if God could only get us there—what wonderful things He could do in our lives!

Child of God, you must be in a position of humility. When you are, God can take you from there and exalt you to the place of His anointing. Humility must come first.

Chapter 2
Knowing the Reality of the Anointing

"Now unto him that is able to do exceeding, abundantly above all that we ask or think, according to the power that worketh in us." **Ephesians 3:20**

What *is* the anointing? That may sound like a basic, perhaps even elementary, question, but until recently, I didn't know the answer myself!

It's a peculiar thing, despite how much we talk, preach and sing about the anointing, very few believers understand it. We *think* we do, of course, but in most cases, what little understanding we have can be summed up by what I call *"The Ooooh, Aaaaah Doctrine."* According to the *Ooooh, Aaaaah Doctrine*, anyone with the anointing must drop their voice an octave and do their best Kathryn Khulman impression. They must drag out all their words and fall into a trance-like state in order to appear spiritual. The idea is that the anointing, if it is real, must create a reaction of awe and amazement at the supernatural. It must be something so distant, deep and unattainable that it appears only great ministers and prophets of God can ever operate in it. Chosen one, this is absolutely not the case. The anointing is for you. It is designed to equip you for everyday life and it is attainable by every born-again believer. All you need is some understanding in order to begin living in it.

So, let's set the *Ooooh, Aaaaah Doctrine* aside and look at what the Word says about the anointing. Let's begin with **John 14:26.** There, Jesus is talking to His disciples during the days just before His crucifixion. He says,

But the Comforter, which is the Holy Ghost, whom the Father will send in my name, He shall teach you

all things, and bring all things to your remembrance, whatsoever I have said unto you.

Jesus tells us here that the Comforter, the Holy Ghost, is a "He." The Holy Spirit is not an "it" or a "thing". He is a person, the third person of the Trinity. Jesus said that when He comes, He shall teach us all things and lead us into all truth (John 16:13).

How is He going to do that? Through an "unction" or "an anointing." **First John 2:20** and **27** tells us:

But ye have an unction from the Holy One, and ye know all things.

. . .The anointing which ye have received of him abideth in you, and ye need not that any man teach you: but as the same anointing teacheth you of all things, and is truth, and is no lie, and even as it hath taught you, ye shall abide in him.

Notice the striking similarity between Jesus' description of the Comforter and John's description of the anointing. According to these scriptures, they both are in us; they both teach us all things; and they both show us truth.

When I discovered this connection, I asked God, "What is happening here? Are the anointing and the Holy Spirit one and the same. Or are they different? How do they fit together?"

What God showed me was this: **The Holy Spirit is a person and the anointing is His personality!**

One definition of the word "person" is the frame or outer make-up of something; the casing. When referring to a human being, the frame is the structure or bodily shape.

The personality, on the other hand, is what actually makes up the person. It is the substance that makes the person who he or she is. For example, God made the person or framework of Adam from the dust of the earth (Genesis 2). But Adam had no substance or personality until God breathed the breath of life into that slab of flesh. It was at that moment, the Bible says, that man became a living soul.

In much the same way, the Holy Ghost is the person or frame, and the anointing is the personality or substance that fills in His frame.

Painted With Power

With that fact in mind, let's take a look at the words "anointing" and "unction" in I John 2:20 and 27. Both of them come from the same Greek word, "charisma", meaning a smearing, rubbing or endowment. It literally means to smear on, overshadow or paint over. The anointing is an endowment of the inherent characteristics, qualities and virtues of the Holy Spirit.

The anointing, when it comes on you, is the painting or smearing of everything that makes up the Holy Ghost directly onto your natural being. It is His personality overshadowing you, clothing you with His virtues, His character and His power rather than your own.

When the "super" of the third person of the Trinity is smeared on your "natural" self, you suddenly become "supernatural". Whatever you previously did by your own natural ability, you now do supernaturally, or above all natural ability.

When I was in school, my science teacher taught me that "power" was the ability to get results. Transfer that definition to the spiritual realm, and you could say *the anointing is God's power to get results in your life.* That means if you're a singer, once the anointing of the Holy Ghost comes upon you, you don't "just" sing anymore; You now sing outstandingly with marvelous results.

If you are a minister, after you've been clothed and painted with the anointing, you minister outstandingly.

In fact, housewives, ushers, businessmen, athletes, musicians, pastors, students, teachers, construction workers—anyone!—who will get into the position to be smeared with the anointing can produce outstanding results.

You see, contrary to popular belief, not everyone who is a winner had to sweat in order to win. Sure, for some people it may require a lot of work to do an assignment, but for someone who is clothed with the power to get results, it happens sweatlessly and with excellence.

The anointing of the Holy Ghost guarantees victory at all times. It is the source of power for every Christian and, tragically, it is the element most frequently missing from our daily lives.

How does its absence affect us? Think of it this way. If I have a microphone, and know how to use it, when I turn it on and speak into it, I expect my voice to be amplified. If, however, someone cuts off the electricity powering it, despite all my knowledge and sound equipment, I'm not going to get an amplified voice. Why? Because, when there is no power flowing, there will be no results.

Two Christians can have the same faith, know the same scriptures and have the same goal—yet one will succeed and the other will fail. They both have all the right spiritual equipment, yet only the one with the power running through his life - the power of the anointing - will get the job done.

When the Impossible Becomes Possible

The Bible is full of examples that illustrate how the power of the Holy Ghost actually works. Take Genesis 1:2 for instance:

And the earth was without form and void; and darkness was upon the face of the deep. And the Spirit of God moved upon the face of the waters.

This verse depicts the Holy Spirit moving on (overshadowing) the face of the waters. We are given the visual impression that He is ready and poised to bring the words of creation to pass.

The earth was formless and empty, yet because the smearing of the Holy Ghost was present, the ability to literally make something out of nothing was there. When God spoke the words **"Let there be light (Genesis 1:3),"** the very muscle of God, in the person of the Holy Ghost, carried those words from the spiritual realm into the physical. The overshadowing of the Holy Ghost gave results to the words of the Father.

Luke chapter one provides another clear example of the Holy Spirit overshadowing and painting His power on someone in order to get results in the natural realm. There, the angel Gabriel delivered some amazing information to Mary, the future mother of Jesus. He said:

And behold, thou shalt conceive in thy womb, and bring forth a son, and shalt call his name JESUS.

He shall be great and shall be called the Son of the Highest: and the Lord God shall give unto him the throne of his father David:

And he shall reign over the house of Jacob for ever; and of his kingdom there shall be no end. (Luke 1:31-33)

This announcement came as great news to Mary except for one small detail:

Then said Mary unto the angel, How shall this be, seeing I know not a man? (verse 34)

To Mary, this looked like an impossible situation. She knew that without the seed of a man, there can be no conception in a woman. Virgins simply don't get pregnant. But look at what Gabriel told her in verse 35:

And the angel answered and said unto her, The Holy Ghost shall come upon thee, and the power of the Highest shall overshadow thee: therefore also that holy thing which shall be born of thee shall be called the Son of God.

He gave Mary a clear and simple explanation as to how this impossible thing would become possible: the **power** of the Highest shall **overshadow** thee.

The overshadowing power that comes from the Holy Ghost is the power of the anointing.

The 16th chapter of John gives us yet another, somewhat different, example of what the anointing can do. In the 12th verse, we find Jesus telling his disciples that there were things that He wanted to reveal to them but couldn't until the Holy Spirit came. Why couldn't He? Because the revelations He wanted to give them were too great for their natural minds to receive. Since the Holy Ghost had not yet come, the disciples couldn't conceive them.

After Pentecost, all that changed. The Holy Ghost came and brought the disciples the power to make the impossible possible. His anointing gave them the power to conceive. As I John 2:27 says, He taught them all things!

Conception Is Guaranteed

Like Mary or the disciples, a delivering Word of the Lord may come to you when you're facing impossible circumstances. You may not understand how it can come to pass, but don't despair. All you need is the smearing of the Holy Ghost! He will guarantee your victory!

You may be in the midst of a financial crisis when the Lord says to you, **"I shall supply all your needs according to my abundant riches in glory. . ." (Philippians 4:19).** At first, you may think, "How shall this thing be, seeing I don't have a job?" But remember, when the power to get results arrives on the scene, the impossible becomes possible.

What "impossibilities" are facing you today? Mary needed conception in her womb if what God had spoken was going to come to pass. You may need conception in your ministry, your home, your business, your finances or your children. You can't make it happen in your own power. If you will lay aside your own knowledge, plans and good ideas, however, and humble yourself under God's hand, conception is guaranteed. Why? Because you are clothed with and overshadowed by the ability to get results. You have the anointing! You have victory!

The Power Within

I know some of the circumstances you're facing may seem overwhelming. I know you may feel like you don't have enough money, strength or education to turn them around. But believe me, you have everything you'll ever need. It has all been deposited on the inside of you in the person of the Holy Ghost. His personality, His supernatural power to get results, is residing in you now, making available to you everything God promised in His Word.

So don't look outside for help, look inside **"to him that is able to do exceeding abundantly above all that we ask or think, *according to the power that worketh in us"* (Ephesians 3:20).**

If you want to see just how much it can do through you, look at what it did for Jesus' first disciples. He told them in **Luke 24:49:**

And, behold, I send the promise of my Father upon you: but tarry ye in the city of Jerusalem, until ye be endued with power from on high.

The promise Jesus was referring to was the Holy Ghost. He said that when the Spirit came upon them, they would be endued with power. To be *endued* means *to be dressed or clothed with the virtues or qualities of the person from which the endowment is coming.*

In other words, the disciples were going to be clothed with the very strength and might of the Holy Spirit. All that He is was about to be smeared on them.

What were they to do once that endowment took place? **Acts 1:8** says they were to "...**be witnesses unto me (Jesus) both in Jerusalem, and in all Judaea, and in Samaria, and unto the uttermost part of the earth."**

Think about that! These men had been assigned the awesome task of taking the Gospel to the entire world. They had to do it without the aid of television, telephones, airplanes or any other modern technical wonders. And, what's more, a third of the world had not even been discovered yet!

Impossible? For the natural man, yes. But when you are painted with the ability to get results (the anointing), there is no obstacle that cannot be overcome, no need that cannot be met and no foe that cannot be defeated.

The disciples demonstrated that fact. They got their impossible job done! You and I are living proof of it.

Don't Leave Home Without It

I said it before and I'm going to say it again: *The anointing is your guaranteed victory!*

The Word alone cannot bring you true victory. When God made the earth, He spoke it into existence with words, yet nothing came forth until there was movement by the Holy Spirit.

The angel spoke the word to Mary, but there could be no pregnancy until the overshadowing of the Spirit came.

Jesus was the Word made flesh. Although He was literally the walking Word, He could do no miracles until the Holy Spirit descended upon Him giving Him power. That's why we have no record of Jesus doing any miracles as a child. Before the Holy Ghost came upon Him, He was only The Word (John I). After his baptism, however, He was The Christ, the Anointed One.

Every Christian needs this smearing of power. That includes you! If the anointing is not present in your life, everything you do will be void of the results God desires you to have. You can speak to mountains, situations and demonic forces all you want, but without the power of the Holy Ghost in your life, you will never see results.

So tap into the anointing, not just a little, but a lot. Be like the Psalmist who said, **"Thou preparest a table before me in the presence of mine enemies: thou anointest my head with oil; my cup runneth over." (Psalm 23:5)**

As in all of scripture, the oil in Psalm 23:5 is symbolic of the anointing of the Holy Spirit. The Psalmist tells us his cup is running over. The cup represents our born-again spirit. He's saying, My spirit is running over with the anointing.

We know, according to God's Word, that as born-again believers the anointing already abides within us. But God wants us to have our cups running over. He wants the anointing to be running out of us. When we lay hands on the sick, the anointing should spill out of our cups onto them and bring healing. When we go to work, God's ability should overflow onto all that we do and make it outstanding.

When I say *outstanding*, I mean it in the strongest possible sense. We should be outstanding like Elisha was outstanding. He walked in so much anointing that months after he was dead and buried, they put another dead man in his tomb and **"when the dead man was let down, and touched the bones of Elisha, he revived, and stood up on his feet." (II Kings 13:21)** That's what I call, "running over"!

The apostle Peter would walk down the street and people would be supernaturally healed by the power to get results that flowed out of him. (See Acts 5:15-16.) The apostle Paul was so full of the anointing that he could deposit it into natural objects and those objects would get results! **Acts 19:12** says, **"From his body were brought unto the sick handkerchiefs or aprons, and the diseases departed from them, and the evil spirits went out of them."**

On many occasions the Bible says "virtue" flowed out of Jesus and healed people. That virtue was the anointing that flowed consistently out of his cup.

Do you think these stories about people like Elisha, Peter, Paul and Jesus are in the Bible just so we can clap our hands in church and get excited over them? No! They were put in there so we could see what the anointing of God can do. They were put in there because the Father has given us that same anointing!

I don't know about you, but I want to operate powerfully in the anointing. I am not going to be content until I pass by someone in the grocery store and they fall out under the power of God.

Listen, you are the new Ark of the Covenant! You are the 1990's model! Full of the Holy Ghost and power!

Are you ready to get that power flowing? Keep reading. You're about to find out how.

Chapter 3
Wisdom and Might:
Ingredients in God's Anointing

"For this cause we also, since the day we heard it, do not cease to pray for you, and to desire that ye might be filled with the knowledge of his will in all wisdom and . . . strengthened with all might, according to his glorious power. . . ." **Colossians 1:9-11**

Now that you know God's anointing is simply the personality of the Holy Ghost, you're probably wondering exactly what that personality is like. Is it made up of many different facets? Does it have distinctive traits like human personalities do?

The answer is "Yes!" In fact, those various facets and traits are what work together to give you your "sweatless" triumph. You will find a list of them in **Isaiah 11:1-3.**

And there shall come forth a rod out of the stem of Jesse, and a Branch shall grow out of his roots:

And the spirit of the Lord shall rest upon him, the spirit of wisdom and understanding, the spirit of counsel and might, the spirit of knowledge and of the fear of the Lord;

And shall make him of quick understanding in the fear of the Lord: and he shall not judge after the sight of his eyes, neither reprove after the hearing of his ears.

This passage identifies seven spirits that make up the personality of the Holy Ghost:

1. The spirit of the Lord
2. The spirit of wisdom

3. The spirit of understanding
4. The spirit of counsel
5. The spirit of might
6. The spirit of knowledge
7. The spirit of the fear of the Lord

All of these are ingredients of the personality of the Holy Spirit. They work together to give you the power to get results. They all aid in bringing about your victory.

Each one is important, of course, but there are two ingredients, I believe, that stand out from among the others. Throughout the Bible, these two are seen giving people victory and results. They are the *spirit of wisdom* and *the spirit of might*. I call them the "Dynamic Duo", because when they are in operation together they cannot be stopped.

When Jesus operated in these areas of the anointing, He experienced phenomenal results. In one instance, it kept Him from being thrown off a cliff by the people of His hometown. They were angry with Jesus because He had just finished preaching a provoking sermon to them. In that sermon, He said He was the fulfillment of the messianic prophesies. In short, he had declared; The Messiah is standing before you. And I am He.

This pronouncement made the people furious. "Who is this carpenter who thinks he can make such claims? He's just Mary and Joseph's boy!" the mob probably roared.

And all they in the synagogue, when they heard these things, were filled with wrath, And rose up, and thrust him out of the city, and led him unto the brow of the hill whereon their city was built, that they might cast him down headlong.

But he passing through the midst of them went his way. (Luke 4:28-30)

Isn't that amazing? Were you or I in that situation, we would probably be screaming, fighting and pleading. Jesus, however, said nothing. He simply turned around, walked through the crowd and went back to doing what God had called Him to do.

Jesus overcame them in a "sweatless" way. How? By the wisdom of God. He didn't react the way we would have or the way our logic would dictate. Instead, He reacted the way the Holy Spirit instructed him to react. The spirit of wisdom gave Jesus the ability to win in spite of the apparently overwhelming odds.

Outsmarted Again

You can see the spirit of wisdom at work in Jesus' life again when the Pharisees brought a woman to Him who had been caught in adultery. They were trying to catch Him in a snare by getting Him to make a judgment on her punishment. They said:

Master, this woman was taken in adultery, in the very act.

Now Moses in the law commanded us, that such should be stoned: but what sayest thou?

This they said, tempting him, that they might have to accuse him. But Jesus stooped down, and with his finger wrote on the ground, as though he heard them not. (John 8:4-6)

Knowing that Jesus was a compassionate, forgiving man and that He would not endorse her execution, these Pharisees were hoping to trick Him into saying something contrary to the law of Moses. If He did, they could then announce to everyone that he was a false teacher who was opposed to the law.

Jesus, however, had the anointing. As a result, he knew what his enemies were up to, and simply remained silent. Because of the spirit of wisdom, He knew not to say a word until He received instructions from the Spirit of God.

Child of God, a problem with many Christians is that they don't shut their mouths and wait to hear what God would have them do. They automatically speak and cause great problems with their hasty words. When you have the spirit of wisdom, you don't say anything until you've heard from heaven. That's what Jesus did. And just look at the result:

So when they continued asking him, he lifted himself, and said unto them, He that is without sin among you, let him first cast a stone at her.

And again he stooped down, and wrote on the ground.

And they which heard it, being convicted by their own conscience, went out one by one, beginning at the eldest, even unto the last: and Jesus was left alone, and the woman standing in the midst. (John 8:7-9)

What marvelous wisdom! You or I could have sat there a million years and never thought of that reply.

It doesn't matter how difficult the situation seems. When you're hooked up to the power to get results, you don't have to worry about coming up with a solution. You will always have the knowledge provided for you in order to win. It will be supernaturally supplied by the spirit of wisdom residing in the anointing!

A Runaway Victory

The other half of the "Dynamic Duo" is the spirit of might. Jesus walked in it all the time. Look at **Matthew 14:1-2.**

At that time Herod the tetrarch heard of the fame of Jesus.

And said unto his servants, This is John the Baptist; he is risen from the dead; and therefore mighty works do shew forth themselves in him.

Because of the presence of the anointing, Jesus did "mighty works." Or, as another translation says, "works of might". Might is *an inherent strength to accomplish or perform*. It is literally the ability to do the impossible. "The Spirit of Might" is God's ability on you to do what only He can do.

Strength and power are components of might, but might goes far beyond them to give you victory over the seemingly impossible. I Chronicles 29:10-12 verifies that this "might" truly is an ingredient of the anointing. It says:

Wherefore David blessed the Lord before all the congregation: and David said, . . .

O Lord, and thou art exalted as head above all.

Both riches and honour come of thee, and thou reignest over all; and in thine hand is power and might; and in thine hand it is to make great, and to give strength unto all.

Might is in God's hand. You will remember in chapter one we discovered that when we humble ourselves before God, we move into a position under His hand. According to this scripture, might is in that same place: Under the hand of God. It is there you will find the strength to accomplish the impossibilities that face you.

Just *how much* might can you find there? More than you can imagine. Look at the life of the prophet Elijah, for example. He was a mere human being just like you or me. However, when the hand of God was upon him, amazing things happened.

On one occasion in Elijah's ministry, he decreed to King Ahab that a three-and-a-half year drought was about to end, and told him to get in his chariot and hurry back to the city because it was about to rain. So Ahab mounted his chariot and horses and headed straight for the city. Now, as a king, Ahab had the best and fastest horses and equipment in the land. He was definitely traveling toward the city with great speed. But look at what Elijah did:

And the *hand of the Lord* was on Elijah; and he girded up his loins, and ran before Ahab to the entrance of Jezreel. (I Kings 18:46)

The hand of the Lord on Elijah caused him to outrun the fastest and best fleet of chariots in the nation of Israel. Now *that's* might!

Through the might of God, Elijah accomplished the impossible. You can do the same thing if you will tap into the anointing and its attending spirit of might. At this point in your life, sickness, poverty or depression may have a head start on you, but if you will exchange your natural ability for the supernatural anointing of God, you can catch these negative circumstances and overtake them. The spirit of might will cause you, like Elijah, to pass those problems and leave them in the dust.

It's for Today!

Some people think that kind of power was just for Old Testament saints. They are wrong. **Ephesians 3:14-16** proves it. There, the apostle Paul writes:

For this cause I bow my knees unto the Father of our Lord Jesus Christ,

Of whom the whole family in heaven and earth is named,

That he would grant you, according to the riches of his glory, to be strengthened with might by his Spirit in the inner man.

Paul was praying that the Ephesians would be strengthened with the ability to accomplish anything. He was praying for them to have the spirit of might. That's not the only time he mentions it either. Ephesians 6:10 says, **"Finally, my brethren, be strong in the Lord, and in the power of his might." Colossians 1:9-11 says:**

For this cause we also, since the day we heard it, do not cease to pray for you, and to desire that ye might be filled with the knowledge of his will in all wisdom and spiritual understanding;

That ye might walk worthy of the Lord unto all pleasing, being fruitful in every good work, and increasing in the knowledge of God; Strengthened with all might, *according to by his glorious power*, unto all patience and longsuffering with joyfulness.

There is no doubt about it, God's might—His strength to accomplish the impossible—is in the anointing. And the anointing is for today!

Keep the Duo Together

Before we can end our discussion about the "Dynamic Duo" of wisdom and might, I want to emphasize that they are a "duo." They operate together. You will rarely find one without the other. Why? Because keeping them together prevents them from being abused.

Let me show you what I mean. Might is the power to do the impossible. If you have might but don't have the wisdom to know how and when to use it, then you will do more damage than you do good.

Some people want a strong anointing just so they can demonstrate how powerful they are. But that's not what the anointing is for! If God gave you might without wisdom, you'd probably use it to win contests of strength and marathon races for your own personal glorification and enrichment. That would be an abuse of divine power. You must have might *and* wisdom.

Wisdom should not be confused with knowledge. They are not the same. Wisdom is the proper application of knowledge. Knowledge alone only puffs up, and is of very little use. High school students, for example, have vast amounts of knowledge stored up, but few of them have any idea of how to use it. It is only when they are given wisdom, or the proper application of that knowledge, that it will ever benefit them.

WHAT YOU DO WITH KNOWLEDGE WILL DETERMINE YOUR SUCCESS OR FAILURE. As **Proverbs 4:7** says, **"Wisdom is the principal (most important) thing; therefore get wisdom."** Once you get it, combine it with might and you'll have an awesome combination that will get you out of very tight spots.

How tight? Ask Daniel. He knew about being in tight spots. Once, he spent the night in a den of lions. (An experience that is definitely outside of most people's comfort zone.) On another occasion, he had to interpret the kings dream—*without knowing what the dream was!* It was an impossible situation, but God's wisdom and might saw him through. **Daniel 2:19-22** tells us:

Then was the secret revealed unto Daniel in a night vision. Then Daniel blessed the God of heaven.

Daniel answered and said, Blessed be the name of God for ever and ever: for wisdom and might are his:

And he changeth the times and the seasons: he removeth kings, and setteth up kings: he giveth wisdom unto the wise, and knowledge to them that know understanding:

He revealeth the deep and secret things: he knoweth what is in the darkness, and the light dwelleth with him.

Wisdom and might: They worked for Elijah. They worked for Daniel. They worked for Jesus. And they will work for you. Seek God for them! Be warned, however. Wisdom and might are not free. They will cost you. They will cost you your independence. They will cost you your pride. But in return you'll receive the power to do the impossible.

Chapter 4
God's Purpose for the Anointing

"Herein is my Father glorified, that ye bear much fruit; so shall ye be my disciples." John 15:8

I have said it previously, but it bears repeating: Very few Christians have a true understanding of the anointing. Most of them just know what they have been taught, and, unfortunately, what they have been taught may not have been exactly right.

They know it involves power, has something to do with the Holy Spirit and that wonderful things are supposed to come as a result of it, but that's about it. In this case the old saying is correct, "A little knowledge is a dangerous thing." A bit of knowledge about something like the anointing can be more dangerous than no knowledge at all.

If I have a large stick of dynamite in my hand, for instance, and all I know about it is that when I hold a match to the end of the fuse it is going to catch on fire and get gradually shorter, I'm in bad shape. Why? Because, acting on that bit of knowledge without understanding the results is dangerous. I need to understand the purpose for which dynamite is intended. If I don't, I might put it in little Johnny's birthday cake and use it as a candle. Then, both the birthday cake and little Johnny will be in trouble.

Likewise, a limited understanding concerning the nature and function of the anointing can be very costly. You hold within you a stick of spiritual dynamite. There are proper and improper uses for it. A limited knowledge of those uses could lead you to seriously abuse it. Therefore, if God is ever going to be able to operate through you as he wants, *you must come to understand God's purpose for the anointing.*

For God's Glory Alone

Although there are many possible uses for the anointing, there is only one legitimate purpose. That purpose is God's purpose. The anointing is to be used for His glorification.

The anointing is not to be used to show how wonderful and spiritual you are. It is not to impress others with the amount of power you possess or the number of miracles you can produce. (Remember, the devil's servants do signs and miracles too. See Exodus 7:9-12.)

The anointing is to be used to glorify the Father and the Son. Jesus said in John 16:14 that when the Holy Ghost came, he would not glorify Himself, but would glorify the Son. Since we know from Hebrews 13:8 that God doesn't change—He is "the same yesterday, today, and forever"—we can rest assured that the Holy Ghost's aim is still the same.

If you are going to operate in the anointing, you must continually keep your motives consistent with God's. You must constantly remember that your purpose is to glorify the Lord Jesus, not yourself. How? By letting your focus always be, "None of me and all of God. None for my glory and everything for His glory." This attitude goes back to humility which we discussed in chapter one. Without it, you will be abusing God's power.

When you lay aside your will and self-glory seeking, you make room for the Holy Ghost to come in and glorify Jesus through you. That is what the anointing is for.

The Way to Win

The anointing, when used to glorify God, brings great power. The purpose of this power is not simply to produce good singing, good preaching or amazing healings, though these things may come as a result of the anointing. Nor is the purpose to cause you to shake all over and fall out under the power of God, though that may happen too. No, *the true purpose for the anointing is to produce victory in your life so that God may be glorified in the earth.*

The power the Holy Ghost brings with Him is for winning. Your Heavenly Father, through the Holy Spirit, has provided the necessary power for you to have "sweatless" victory in your life. This brings Him glory.

If you want to win and be an overcomer, then you must be clothed with the anointing. It will give you victory regardless of what impossibilities face you.

Impossible situations are an inevitable part of each of our lives. We are often defeated because we attempt to fight these situations in our own power and ability. This is tragic because the power to win is residing inside of us. This familiar passage of scripture illustrates this point.

And the angel who talked with me came again and awakened me, like a man who is wakened out of his sleep.

And said to me, What do you see? I said, I see, and behold, a lampstand all of gold, with its bowl [for oil] on the top of it and its seven lamps on it, and [there are] seven pipes to each of the seven lamps which are upon the top of it.

And there are two olive trees by it, one upon the right side of the bowl and the other upon the left side of it [feeding it continuously with oil].

So I asked the angel who talked with me, What are these, my Lord?

Then the angel who talked with me answered me, Do you not know what these are? And I said, No, my lord.

Then he said to me, This [addition of the bowl to the candlestick, causing it to yield a ceaseless supply of oil from the olive trees] is the word of the

Lord to Zerubabel, saying, Not by might, not by power, but by my Spirit [of Whom the oil is a symbol], says the Lord of hosts. (Zechariah 4:1-6 Amp.)

There is a lot of truth in this passage of scripture. First and foremost, it tells you that the way to have victory in your life is not through your own power, but rather through the power of the Holy Ghost. Simply stated, without the anointing you cannot win. If you don't have the anointing, then your home, job, school or ministry will never experience **God's true success**. True victory in the life of a Christian is not a product of education, knowledge, popularity or crafty maneuvering. It comes only from the oil of the Holy Ghost. Oil is representative of the anointing, and without a continuous supply of oil (verse 3) there can be no continuous victory.

Not Just Form But Power!

It's not enough to have the form of a winner. You must have the power to win as well. This has been one of the Church's biggest problems. Many have been doing things in form only. They walk, talk, read, speak in tongues and carry their Bibles just like real anointed Christians. But it's all just a form of godliness. Those things are just techniques, good in and of themselves, but lacking the power to deliver true victory.

For example, you may be constantly confessing that you are the head and not the tail (Deuteronomy 28:13). Don't misunderstand, that's a great thing to be doing, but if you don't have the power of the Holy Ghost operating in your life, you will be overcome more and more every day.

It is a senseless tragedy to have the ability to get results inside you, yet fail to tap into it! You constantly operate in a form of godliness but deny the power thereof (II Timothy 3:5). Beloved, it does not have to be that way.

You can have success and "sweatless" victory if you would only tap into the anointing. It was created to give you power and victory in your life so God will be glorified. Yes, the anointing brings results. Nevertheless, some people are so focused on the outward display and appearance that accompanies the Holy Ghost's power that they miss the victory He so earnestly desires to give them.

The anointing is good for so much more than chills, goose bumps and falling down. However, many people become content when these things start happening to them, thinking that they have experienced all the anointing has to offer. The sad truth is, they often continue their lives in bondage to many things.

You may go to a powerful service at your church in which the pastor prays for people to be delivered from bad habits. You can have him pray for you, and you can even fall on the floor. What good is that if, when you get up, you are still in the same bondage you were in before you fell down? You have experienced the outward display but missed the inward deliverance! You did not experience the true anointing of the Holy Ghost!

The acid test for whether you have really experienced the anointing can be summed up in one statement: *When you come in contact with the anointing of God, it not only affects your moment, it affects your tomorrow.* When you come in contact with the anointing, there will always be a change in your life!

Operate with Excellence

You'll find everything you could ever want or need when you place yourself under the control of the Holy Ghost. If you need healing, you already have it in the anointing. If you need prosperity, it's yours in the anointing. Joy, deliverance and anything else you could ever need is there.

As **II Peter 1:3** says, **"God . . . according to His divine power hath given us all things that pertain unto life and godliness."** That divine power is the anointing that dwells in us in the person of the Holy Ghost.

If you want to see a Biblical illustration of the power and blessings that come with the anointing, read I Samuel 10. It tells us much about the anointing. In verse one, we see Saul being anointed by Samuel to be King over Israel.

Then Samuel took a vial of oil, and poured it upon his head, and kissed him, and said, Is it not because the Lord hath anointed thee to be captain over his inheritance?

In the Old Testament, no one ever took an office of authority without first being anointed with oil. It was that anointing that provided *the ability to operate with excellence in that office.*

The anointing works the same way today. If you are called to be a pastor, then God is responsible for giving you all of the necessary equipment to pastor with excellence. If you are called to be an usher, then you have the ability to usher flawlessly. That may sound strange, but it's true. It would not be fair of God to ask someone to do something that He did not give them the ability to do.

When a person is hooked up and fully submitted to the anointing, they will do everything they are called to do, and do it perfectly.

The anoin'ing gives you the resources to get where you are called to ɔe and to do what you are called to do. It will place you in your *correct* position in life.

Many people want to pick and choose what office they would like to be in. There is no humility in that, and as we have seen, where there is no humility, there is no anointing.

Restoration and "Frontsliding"

Another product of the anointing is *restoration*. We see it in I Samuel 10:2 when the prophet Samuel tells young Saul that the lost donkeys he had been seeking for his father had been found. He said:

When thou art departed from me to day, then thou shalt find two men by Rachel's sepulchre in the border of Benjamin at Zelzah; and they will say unto thee, The asses which thou wentest to seek are found: and, lo, thy father hath left the care of the asses, and sorroweth for you, saying, What shall I do for my son?

Perhaps you, like Saul, have lost something. You may have lost your dignity, your strength, your family, your friends, your hope or even your will to live. Whatever it is, you can experience supernatural restoration if you'll get hooked into the anointing. Whatever is missing in your life will be restored to you once you have been smeared and painted with the power of the Holy Spirit.

Verse three reveals yet another exciting product of the anointing—progress!

Then shalt thou *go on forward* from thence, and thou shalt come to the plain of Tabor, and there shall meet thee three men going up to God to Bethel, one carrying three kids, and another carrying three loaves of bread, and another carrying a bottle of wine.

The anointing will give you the ability to make supernatural progress. When you are anointed, you go forward, not backward. In everything from your finances to your walk with Christ you should be going forward and getting bigger and better.

The Bible says that we should move from faith to faith and glory to glory in all areas of our lives. God has not called you to backslide, He has called you to "frontslide." If you are not moving upward, then you need to get plugged into the power socket. The anointing gives the power to go forward.

Supernatural Favor

We discover still another benefit of the anointing in verse 4.

And they will <u>salute thee</u>, and <u>give thee</u> two loaves of bread; which thou shalt receive of their hands.

Here we see that the anointing produces favor. When the favor of God is upon you, it causes you to receive things you have not even requested. Saul had not asked for bread, these people simply gave it to him. Because the anointing was speaking for him, he did not *have* to ask.

The anointing will speak for you and I in the same way. For example, if you want to fly on a particular flight, but the ticket agent says the flight is booked, there is no need to worry. You have the favor of God working for you. Not only will you get a seat, but it will be in first class! Glory to God!

Or, if the company you work for is laying people off left and right, the anointing will not only cause you to keep your job, it will get you a promotion! Because you are connected to the source of guaranteed victory, you cannot lose!

I will never forget the time I was believing God for a car. I walked into a bank and said, "I want a loan for a BMW." After looking at my credentials for a while, the loan officer pointed her finger in my face and said, "You will never get money for this car! No one in this city will give it to you!"

Her attitude made me mad. To be honest, I almost got in the flesh and said, "Don't you put your hand in my face lady!" But I thank God for temperance. Instead, I looked at her right in the eye and said, "Lady, I will have my car." I went to another bank and was told the same thing. "It will never happen," they said. Nevertheless, I didn't stop, because the favor of the Lord was working for me.

Now just prior to this time, I had co-signed a little $500.00 loan for someone to help them out. When I got the papers back, however, they told me I owed $1,000.00! I had been ripped off!

You know, of course, how easy it is to get upset when people start messing with your money. But the Lord told me that if I would forgive that person's debt, He would give me favor. So, I consented and released them completely.

Now, I had only one day left to get the loan before the BMW I wanted was sold. So, I went into a credit union and said, "Do you think you could loan me some money to buy a car?" They informed me that I was at a Federal Aviation Administration credit union and that I would have to be a member to borrow money. What's more, I had to be a pilot or an FAA employee to join. "I'm sorry, we can't help you," I was told. So I went home.

I was not discouraged, however, because the Holy Ghost had already spoken for me. When I got home, the phone rang. The voice on the other end said, "This is Mr.

Davis from the FAA. I'm calling to tell you that I checked our records and, apparently, you are already a member of this credit union."

"Wait a minute," I said, "How did I get to be a member of the FAA credit union?"

"Well," he asked, "Have you co-signed on a note for someone recently?"

"Yes, I have," I told him, remembering my unpleasant experience.

"Well, the person you co-signed for is one of our members, and when you co-signed for her, you automatically became a member. If you'll come back today, I see no reason why we can't take care of your car loan or anything else you might need."

Needless to say, I was shocked, but this is precisely the kind of thing that happens when the favor of the Lord is working on your behalf. When the Holy Ghost is speaking for you, it does not matter what the devil says or what your circumstances look like. You are going to get what you desire, because the favor of God is on the scene!

Good-bye, Clark Kent/Hello, Superman!

Let's look once again at Saul's experience just after being anointed by Samuel. In verses 5 and 6 of I Samuel chapter 10 we read:

After that thou shalt come to the hill of God, where is the garrison of the Philistines: and it shall come to pass, when thou art come thither to the city, that thou shalt meet a company of prophets coming down from the high place with a psaltery, and a tabret, and a pipe, and a harp, before them; and they shall prophesy:

And the *Spirit of the Lord* will come *upon* thee, and thou shalt prophesy with them, <u>and shalt be turned into another man</u>.

Did you catch that last phrase, "You shall be changed into another man"?

When the anointing comes on you, there will be a **change of status.** You will not be the same person you used to be, because you now have a different personality operating through you. It does not matter what kind of person you are right now, when the Holy Spirit has an opportunity to paint and smear you with his personality, there will be a change of status. You will no longer be the on the lowest rung of the corporate ladder at work, you will be the CEO.

When the anointing comes on you you're not Clark Kent anymore, you're Superman, with the ability to do all things. Philippians 4:13 says that you can do all things through Christ, meaning the Anointed One, that strengthens you. Glory to God! Think about it. Your body is literally the temple of the Holy Ghost. Therefore, you have the power to do anything! Hallelujah!

This theme of supernatural strength through the anointing is repeated throughout scripture. **Psalm 92:10-11** is one example.

But my horn shalt thou exalt like the horn of an unicorn (literally a wild ox): I shall be anointed with fresh oil.

Mine eye also shall see my desire on my enemies, and mine ears shall hear my desire of the wicked that rise up against me.

The horn in scripture is symbolic of excessive strength. This scripture says that when you have the anointing, you have excessive strength like that of a wild ox. When you get wrapped up in the anointing, you will have strength that no flood or force on earth can overcome.

These verses also tell you that, because of the anointing, you shall see your desire upon your enemies. That is why God tells non-covenant people not to touch His anointed. The anointed are endued with the power to see what they say come to pass on their enemies.

When you are under the anointing of God, you're very dangerous to the kingdom of darkness. You have the power to see whatever you desire come upon the satanic enemies that would ruin the lives of your family and friends.

A Conspiracy Revealed

Also, notice that this verse says you shall hear the plans that the wicked make against you. That means **nothing** shall take you by surprise.

If there is a conspiracy in your ministry, home or office, you will overcome it because the Holy Spirit will show you clearly who is involved and what they are planning. You will never lose, because you have tapped into the source of guaranteed victory.

I have experienced this type of operation in my own life many times. I remember one incident that occurred back before I was pastoring a church of my own. Three women came to my senior pastor and told him that I was a "Judas" and that I was betraying him. I was out of town at the time and had no idea what had taken place.

When I arrived back in town, I was sitting at my desk with my head down when the Lord began to show me a vision. I saw the entire thing. I saw the three women and heard exactly what they had said.

When the vision was over, I jumped up from my desk in great excitement at experiencing one of the gifts of the Holy Spirit in operation. In my excitement, I forgot the implications of what these women had said. I ran into my pastor's office to tell him what God had shown me.

I rushed in and blurted, "Guess what happened! I believe God just showed me a vision, and I want you to tell me if it is right or wrong."

"O.K." my pastor said.

"When I was out of town, three ladies came into your office and told you that I was a 'Judas' and I was trying to betray you. Is that true?" I asked.

My pastor looked at me in amazement, fell back in his chair and said, "That's right! Who told you that?"

I jumped up and said, "It was the Holy Ghost that just told me in a vision. I knew I was right. I knew it! I knew it!"

I was so thrilled at getting such a vivid vision that I had forgotten to be concerned about what the women had said. Then it hit me. I looked at my pastor and said, "They said what about me?!!! I can't believe it!!"

The point is, the Holy Ghost revealed to me a plot that the enemy tried to bring against me and His plan was foiled. That's a blessing of the anointing.

Tall, Strong and Full of Fruit

Here's another benefit of the anointing listed in **Psalm 92:**

The righteous shall flourish like a palm tree, He shall grow like a cedar in Lebanon. Those that be planted in the house of the Lord shall flourish in the courts of our God. They shall still bring forth fruit in old age; they shall be fat and flourishing. (Verses 12-14)

When you are clothed with the anointing, you are like a palm tree. The palm is the last of all trees to submit to harsh weather. Wind, rain, floods and drought cannot move it like the rest of the plants. This means that when you tap into the anointing, regardless of what the circumstances are doing to people around you, you shall stand strong with great resistance.

Verse 12 also says that you will grow like the cedar of Lebanon. The cedar is the tallest tree in Lebanon. This means that once you have the anointing, you will move to new heights supernaturally. You will truly be above only, never beneath again (Deuteronomy 28).

Finally, it says that the anointed ones shall bring forth fruit in old age: they shall be fat and flourishing. Glory to God, even when you are old you will continue to flourish. You will remain productive, profitable and healthy because of the anointing of the Holy Spirit.

Excellence, restoration, progress, favor, elevated status, strength, growth and devil-stomping power—all these benefits come with the anointing. If you don't have them, get them! Get hooked up to the anointing to start seeing the fruit of the Word!

Jesus said in John 15 that the Father is glorified when we bear much fruit. If everyone who reads this book would begin to live under the anointing and start bearing fruit, then the Church as a whole, and as individuals, would experience great victory. And our God, the Lord Jehovah, would be glorified throughout the earth!

Chapter 5
Paying the Price for the Anointing: The Foundation

"The grace of the Lord Jesus Christ, and the love of God, and the communion of the Holy Ghost, be with you all. Amen." **II Corinthians 13:14**

"I want it! I must have the anointing!" That's what your spirit may be shouting right now. If so, that's wonderful because God wants you to have it.

However, there are seven foundational things that must be established in your life before you can ever begin to experience the power of the anointing. They are essential keys to operating in the power to get results.

1. Get under the covering of an anointed ministry.

Association brings assimilation. In other words, the things with which you associate will eventually be assimilated into your life. They will become a part of you. There is an old saying, "If you lie down with dogs, you will get up with fleas." It's true. If you are being fed at a cold, dead church with icicles hanging from the ceiling and polar bears sitting in the congregation, a church that is not teaching the anointed Word of God or giving liberty to the Holy Spirit, you will eventually become a spiritual ice cube yourself—cold, dead and void of the Spirit's life.

It is a fact that if you are not hanging around the anointing, you will not pick up the anointing. If, on the other hand, you draw close to the fire of the Holy Ghost, you'll eventually be on fire. It's unavoidable.

God will call you to a particular church to help carry out a particular vision. It is vitally important that you obey Him and get to the place that He has called you to be. There and only there will all of your needs be met.

In I Kings 17:3-6 God told the prophet Elijah to go to a certain brook. It was at that particular brook that Elijah's needs were supernaturally met in a time of famine. Just as God chose that brook for Elijah, He has chosen a certain church where He wants you to serve. When you get to that place, you will find that your needs are consistently met.

Perhaps you are faced with a difficult decision and you are unsure of what direction to go in. Wouldn't it be a blessing if you went to church on Sunday and your pastor "just happened" to say something that eased your decision or gave you direction as to what to do? This is a wonderful thing, but it can only happen when you are where God has called you to be.

Child of God, listen, if you are presently attending a church where you feel as though nothing that is said applies to you, you are probably in the wrong place. So get out—and get to the place where you can be fed and nourished as God desires!

"But Brother Dollar, you don't understand. My grandmother has been at this church for 65 years! My uncle founded it! All my cousins were married in it! If I leave, they'll all be so mad at me they won't speak to me anymore!"

That does not matter! You cannot afford to be in bondage to what people think. It is better to have people mad at you than to be out of God's will. It is better to obey the voice of the Lord than to be held captive by the voices of men.

Do you want the anointing? Then go where the anointing is present and the Word is being taught! Make it your first priority to get under the covering of an anointed ministry.

2. Develop an honest prayer life.

God wants you to be truthful, not religious. He is not concerned with how well you shout "Hallelujah" or how many times you can say "Thank you, Jesus" in one prayer. God is concerned about your heart. God wants to hear from the *real you*, not the *churchy you* religion has created. He wants to have a truly intimate, personal relationship with you. The doorway to that intimacy is honesty. We can see that in **Psalm 145:18.**

The Lord is nigh (near) unto all them that call upon him, to all that call upon him in truth.

God wants to hear the truth from you. If you sow truth to God in your prayer life, the Holy Spirit can lead you into all truth. That harvest of truth will make you free.

Now, there are two types of truth. There is "good-looking" truth and there is "ugly" truth. If you sin, just tell God the ugly truth. Don't try to dress it up and say, "Lord, I kind of—sort of committed fornication a little bit." You cannot "kind of" commit fornication! You either do it or you don't.

Just be honest with God and say, "Lord, I blew it, and I repent." Tell the truth! When you do, God can take the truth of your sin and give you the truth that will get you delivered from that sin. When God gives you that truth, you are made free indeed (John 8:32, 36). Glory to God!

Remember this: God cannot make you free from bondage, whether it be fornication, lying, depression, anger or any other yoke, until you first get honest with Him about the situation. Even though He already knows what has happened, He does not have the liberty to operate in forgiveness and deliverance until you have been completely transparent and humble with Him. You must be honest with God in your prayer life. It is a prerequisite for the anointing.

3. Get a fresh infilling of the Spirit every day.

When it comes to walking in the anointing of God, you must fill your spiritual tanks regularly just as you would the gas tank in your car. When you go too long without refilling your car, it eventually stops running. The same applies to you spiritually.

Every day, you must fill up with the Word, spend time in prayer, spend time in worship and praise and commune with the Holy Spirit. This is a very important part of operating in the anointing. Get a fresh infilling everyday.

4. Repent!

There must be the element of ready repentance in your life if you are to operate in the anointing. Please understand, to repent does not mean you say, "I'm sorry." It means you change. True repentance is a change of heart, a change of mind and a change of direction. Sadly, there are plenty of people telling God they're sorry, but only a precious few truly repenting and changing. You can say that you want to repent; say that you are going to repent; and even say that you have repented, but there has been no true repentance unless there has been change.

A great model for repentance is found in **Luke 18:10-14.**

Two men went up into the temple to pray; the one a Pharisee, and the other a publican.

The Pharisee stood and prayed thus with himself, God, I thank thee, that I am not as other men are, extortioners, unjust, adulterers, or even as this publican.

I fast twice in the week, I give tithes of all that I possess.

And the publican, standing afar off, would not lift up so much as his eyes unto heaven, but smote upon his breast, saying, God be merciful to me a sinner.

I tell you, this man went down to his house justified rather than the other: for every one that exalteth himself shall be abased; and he that humbleth himself shall be exalted.

Here we see God's attitude toward those who repent. He says that the man who exalted himself in pride was abased, or brought low. However, the man who repented for his faults was justified. His humility and repentance brought him to exaltation. Glory to God!

So, learn to repent! If you become aware that you are going in the wrong direction, simply change your direction. Do it immediately! If you don't, Satan will have an opportunity to come in and use his two favorite weapons: guilt and condemnation. He will tell you that you have no business going back into the presence of God. He will tell you that you are unworthy. His accusations will drag you down until you stop praying and reading the Word like you used to. Eventually, you will stop altogether. When that happens you have taken yourself out of a position to be clothed with the anointing—and *that* is exactly what the enemy wants.

Any time you blow it, remember, you have an advocate with the Father and all of your sins have been eternally remitted through the blood of Jesus. Therefore, when you have messed up and gone the wrong way, don't run away from Jesus. Don't stop doing what He has called you to do. Turn around and run to him.

Never stay away from God because of condemnation. The anointing and the Holy Spirit are still available. Don't miss out on them by listening to the devil tell you what an unworthy worm you are. Just repent and get back to God through the cleansing blood of Jesus. Then, continue doing what He has called you to do.

5. Learn to yield to the Holy Spirit.

This is one of the most difficult things for Christians to learn. It is also one of the most important. If the power of God is present to heal or deliver you, but your natural mind resists God's methods, you can fail to receive His blessing.

Sometimes, for instance, when the anointing of God is present in a service and people begin to fall out under His power, some will try to stop themselves because they do not want to look foolish in front of other people. In so doing, they hinder the power of God's anointing. There may have been something God wanted to say or do to them while they were out under His power, but they miss it because of their failure to yield.

There are two different kinds of yielding: One is to God and the other, to Satan. **Romans 6:13, 16** mentions both of them.

Neither yield ye your members as instruments of unrighteousness unto sin: but yield yourselves unto God, as those that are alive from the dead, and your members as instruments of righteousness unto God.

Know ye not, that to whom ye yield yourselves servants to obey, his servants ye are to whom ye obey; whether of sin unto death, or of obedience unto righteousness?

People have very little trouble yielding themselves to the power of sin. All they have to do is make a decision and act on it. It is not hard for them to drink, smoke, curse or complain. All they need to do is yield to the spirit that is tempting them.

The same principle is true with the anointing. All you have to do is submit to what the Holy Spirit is wanting to do in your life, and act. The key to this, once again, is humility. When you surrender to God your power to do your will, He will give you His power to do His will. Learn how to yield to the anointing of the Holy Spirit.

6. Fellowship with the Holy Spirit.

The sixth thing that must be present in your life in order to experience God's anointing is the communion of the Holy Ghost. Paul refers to it in **II Corinthians 13:14:**

The grace of the Lord Jesus Christ, and the love of God, and the *communion of the Holy Ghost*, be with you all. Amen.

Communion with the Holy Ghost is tremendously important. But what does it mean? The word communion in this verse is translated from the Greek word "koinonia." Koinonia denotes intimate fellowship and sharing. This is precisely what you must do with the Holy Ghost. Spend time with Him. Talk to Him. Worship Him.

When you do these things, you become sensitive to his voice and presence. Then, you begin to intimately know His power and anointing.

Make communing with the Holy Ghost a priority in your life.

7. Be consistent.

The final thing anyone who wants to operate in the anointing must have is consistency. You must consistently make the previous six items a part of your daily life. By doing so, you lay the foundation for the power to get results to consistently flow and operate in your life. It is important to remember that consistency is the key to the breakthrough (John 8:31-32). If you do not see results immediately, do not stop. Continue on until you receive what God has promised!

Consistency keeps the foundation for the anointing together.

Chapter 6
Paying the Price for the Anointing: The Purchase

"O God, thou art my God; early will I seek thee: my soul thirsteth for thee, my flesh longeth for thee in a dry and thirsty land" **Psalm 63:1**

Now that we have established the foundation, we are ready to move on to the actual purchase. *"Purchase?"* you ask. Yes! Operating in the anointing is neither free, nor cheap. There is a price to be paid. It requires that you give up something of yourself in order to receive from God.

Many people see Benny Hinn or Kenneth Copeland on television and say, "I want his anointing." However, very few of those people consider the price those men paid for the anointing. Other people go to power-packed services and try on the anointing as if it were a garment in a department store dressing room. There is nothing wrong with trying it on, but understand this: *it will never be yours until you have paid the price for it yourself.* The same principle applies to the anointing.

Are You Thirsty?
Ho, Every one that thirsteth, come ye to the waters, and he that hath no money; come ye, buy, and eat; yea, come, buy wine and milk without money and without price. (Isaiah 55:1)

The first thing you must have in order to make the anointing yours is a thirst for it. You must literally crave the manifestation of the power of God in your life. Then you must come to the waters and buy.

The waters represent the Word. Jesus said out of your spirit shall flow rivers of living water (John 7:38). The Bible says that these waters were from the Holy Spirit who had not been given at that time. But now He is here on the inside of us. Praise God!

If you are thirsty for the anointing, you must go to the waters and buy. The word "buy" is very significant in Isaiah 55. Isaiah did not say, "come to the waters and pick or choose." He said, "**Buy.**" When you buy something, there is an exchange. If you want a candy bar, for example, there must be money given in exchange for it. Something must leave you in order to get it. You must give up in order to receive. You must also "buy" the anointing. No one can buy the anointing for you. Nor can you buy the anointing with money, yet there must be an exchange between you and God.

You will spend hours in fervent prayer. You will give up food in times of fasting. You may give up TV, movies and time with friends and family. In order to quench this thirst, you must be willing to give up everything. But it is worth it all many times over because once you buy, you have it forever.

David had that thirst.

O God, thou art my God; early will I seek thee: my soul thirsteth for thee, my flesh longeth for thee in a dry and thirsty land, where no water is; To see thy power and thy glory, so as I have seen thee in the sanctuary. (Psalm 63:1-2)

David proclaims that his soul is thirsty for God and his flesh longs to see God's power manifested as he has seen it in the sanctuary. He wanted to see the miracles that happened at church happen in his personal life.

This should be your attitude as well. You should say, "I'm so thirsty for what you have, God, that I will rise early every morning to seek it. I will do whatever I have to do to receive the fullness of Your anointing. I'll lay on my face for hours in prayer. I'll fast. I'll give up anything that stands between me and Your power."

You may think that sounds extreme. To you, it may be. It all depends on how badly you want to know God's power. When you really want something, you will find a way to get it. You will not accept an excuse for not having it.

When you are ravenously hungry late at night and every restaurant in town seems to be closed, you will not stop looking until you find an open restaurant somewhere. You are determined. *You will find some food.*

You should be the same way about the anointing. If you really want it, you will pay whatever you have to and seek God for it as longs as it takes. In order to put forth that kind of effort, you must be thirsty for it.

If you think that sounds hard, you are right, it is. There is no way around it. If you want to be pure gold, the furnace is your passage. If you want the anointing, the price must be paid.

Let It Rain

"Okay," you say, "I'm willing to pay the price, but where do I start?" You'll find your answer is in **Zechariah 10:1.**

Ask ye of the Lord rain in the time of the latter rain; so the Lord shall make bright clouds, and give them showers of rain, to every one grass in the field.

Rain is a symbol of the anointing and outpouring of the Holy Spirit. Ask for the rain. If you do not have the anointing of God operating on your job, ask for it. If you do not have the anointing of God to get your body healed, ask for it. We are told to ask in the time of the "latter rain." We are living in that time.

Child of God, all you have to do is take this scripture and go before God and say, "Lord, give me the anointing. I ask for the rain. I ask for the anointing in my life." If you do this, He will cause the showers to come. Those showers are the anointing and all the power and blessings that come with it.

Can I Get a Witness?

Once you have begun to pray and release your faith for the anointing, add action to that faith. Begin to stir things up with (1) Thanksgiving, (2) Praise and (3) Testimony. As **Psalm 92:1** says, **"It is a good thing to give thanks unto the Lord, and to sing praises unto thy name, O most High."**

Remember when David was getting ready to fight Goliath? The first thing he did was testify, **"I killed the lion. I killed the bear. Who is this uncircumcised Philistine...?"** (See **I Samuel 17:36**)

His testimony stirred up the anointing inside him. You can do this too. When you receive a bill that you cannot pay, say "I paid the light bill. I paid the gas bill. What is this medical bill...?" Or when sickness comes, say "He healed me of a headache. He healed me of a backache. What is this tumor...?"

Testimony like that stirs up the anointing. When that happens, you have the power to win. That is why John says that we overcome the devil with the blood of the lamb and the word of our testimony. (See Revelation 12:11.) Glory be to God!

I don't care how young or inexperienced you are in the things of God, if you have been born again, you have a testimony to tell, a reason to give thanks and the power to praise. So, get with it—and get ready to overcome!

Chapter 7
Paying the Price for the Anointing: Fasting and Prayer

"Then came the disciples to Jesus apart and said, Why could not we cast him out? And Jesus said unto them, Because of your unbelief... Howbeit this kind goeth not out but by prayer and fasting." **Matthew 17:19-21**

One of the most powerful and effective ways a believer can pay the price for the anointing is through fasting and prayer.

You have very little in life more precious than your time **(prayer)** and your body **(fasting)**. These two items possess a lot of buying power.

It is important to keep in mind that although fasting and prayer are powerful tools, they are not designed to move or change God. They move and change *you*. You can fast four hours or 40 days, and God will not be benefited. You will! Prayer does not help God be who He needs to be, it helps you be who you need to be.

Fasting and prayer go hand in hand. Fasting alone will do nothing more than clean out your digestive system. Even unsaved people fast for this reason. However, when you add the element of prayer to your fast, some wonderful things can happen.

Bringing Your Soul In Line
Fasting brings your flesh and soul into subjection to your spirit-man. It breaks down the will of your carnal flesh and mind so that your born-again spirit can be in control. When your spirit-man is in control, you are in a position to experience God's power, the power of the anointing.

David knew that. Look at **Psalm 69:10.**

When I wept, and chastened my soul with fasting, that was to my reproach.

To "chasten" means to give direction and lead into the right path. Here, David brought his soul (mind) into the right path through fasting. As Christians, the path our minds need to be on is the Word of God. When we fast, we bring our minds and thought patterns in line with the Word of God.

Fasting has another beneficial effect on our soulish man. It "humbles" it.

But as for me, when they were sick, my clothing was sackcloth: I humbled my soul with fasting; and my prayer returned into mine own bosom. (Psalm 35:13)

We can and should humble our souls through fasting. When we fast, we put down our reasonings and rationalizations, and take up the thoughts of God. It puts us in a place of humility, the place where we can be endued with power.

When your mind is in humble subjection to your born-again spirit, you do not make decisions based on your own good ideas. You wait for God's direction. And as long as you follow God's instructions, you cannot lose.

When your soul is humbled through fasting, your prayers will come back to you full of answers and victory. Why? Because you have the anointing, and it is the power to get results.

A Powerful Exchange

When you fast, you give up something. You may give up food, television, physical relations with your spouse or anything else that gratifies an appetite of your flesh, in order to receive from God. Your fasting acts as a medium of exchange for God's power. It does not impress God, but it will place you in a position to be clothed with His power.

On one occasion, Jesus' disciples had been trying, unsuccessfully, to cast an evil spirit out of a young boy. What did Jesus identify as their problem?

Howbeit, this kind goeth not out but by prayer and fasting. (Matthew 17:21)

When Jesus rebuked that spirit, He got instant results. He experienced victory in that situation with very little effort. The reason is simple: Jesus lived a lifestyle of prayer and fasting. He operated in the anointing that assured him "sweatless" victory. His disciples did not.

Surely, they had seen Jesus cast out devils before. They had the right form, said the right words and went through the right motions. However, they failed to go to the waters to make an exchange for power. (See Isaiah 55:1.)

Jesus told the disciples that they could not cast out that devil because that they had made no purchase. They had not paid the price in order to get the faith-power to cast it out. The price Jesus told them to pay was fasting and prayer. Those two things are a key to obtaining the power to make impossibilities possible.

Everyone Has to Pay the Price

Prayer also works as a medium of exchange. Prayer time is time that you give up in order to communicate and fellowship with the Father. There are a million other things you could be doing during that time, but you choose to dedicate that time to God. You give up your plans, purposes and pursuits, and give that time to God. That pleases God, and puts you in a place to receive His power.

If you examine the lives of mighty men and women of God, you will find that before they operated in the anointing, they spent time in fasting and prayer. Moses had a mighty anointing on him. So much so, that people could not look at him in the face. Before he operated in the anointing, he spent forty days and nights fasting and praying, paying the price for that power. He went to the waters and "bought" God's power.

Even Jesus had to pay the price for the anointing. Before the power of God was manifested in Jesus' life, He spent forty days and nights in the wilderness fasting and praying. When He came out, He could do whatever was necessary because He had paid the price for victory.

You will not find one prophet in the Old Testament that carried the anointing of the Holy Ghost who did not first spend time in prayer and fasting. The same is true for the New Testament saints. In **Luke 2:37-38** we see Anna, the prophetess, getting a glimpse of the newborn Messiah.

And she was a widow of about fourscore and four years, which departed not from the temple, but served God with fastings and prayers night and day.

And she coming in that instant gave thanks likewise unto the Lord, and spake of him to all them that looked for redemption in Jerusalem.

Anna served God with fastings and prayers. Her reward? A look into the face of the Savior of the world!

Don't Wait Till "All Else Fails"

Sometimes the decision to fast is a matter of life and death. **Ezra 8:21-22** tells us of such.

Then I (Ezra) proclaimed a fast there, at the river Ahava, that we might afflict ourselves before our God, to seek of him a right way for us, and for our little ones, and for all our substance.

For I was ashamed to require of the king a band of soldiers and horsemen to help us against the enemy in the way: because we had spoken unto the king,

saying, The hand of our God is upon all them for good that seek him; but his power and his wrath is against all them that forsake him.

Ezra and his fellow Jews were about to return to Jerusalem after years of exile in Babylon. They were about to cross many miles of dangerous territory while carrying with them great wealth which was to be used to restore the temple. With such treasure, they were sure to be preyed upon by thieves and bandits. Yet, they had no weapons and no battle plan.

Ezra could not go to the king of Babylon for military help because he had already assured him that God would take care of them. Therefore, they fasted and sought God for a solution to their dilemma. He gave it to them.

Often, we are too quick to seek the help of man instead of the help of God in a time of crisis. We will exhaust all other avenues, then "if all else fails" we will turn to God. Our priorities are upside-down. Matthew 6:33 instructs us to seek God *first* and everything else will be provided.

How did God deliver Ezra and his people out of their predicament? Verse 31 says,

Then we departed from the river Ahava on the twelfth day of the first month, to go unto Jerusalem: and the hand of our God was upon us, and he delivered us from the hand of the enemy, and of such as lay in wait by the way.

The hand of God is symbolic of the anointing. (Remember: It was the hand of God on Elijah that caused him to out-run chariots.) After they fasted and sought God's wisdom, the hand of God was upon them and they were delivered.

They got results! They won! But only after a season of fasting and prayer. They went to the waters to buy.

An Outpouring of Victory

If you are willing to pay the price, you can be delivered from trouble just as Ezra was delivered. You can literally see victory poured out like rain.

Therefore also now, saith the Lord, Turn ye even to me with all your heart, and with fasting, and with weeping, and with mourning:

And rend your heart, and not your garments, and turn unto the Lord your God: for he is gracious and merciful, slow to anger, and of great kindness, and repenteth him of evil

. . . Blow the trumpet in Zion, sanctify a fast

. . . Then will the Lord be jealous for his land, and pity his people.

Yea, the Lord will answer and say unto his people, Behold, I will send you corn, and wine, and oil, and ye shall be satisfied therewith. Be glad then, ye children of Zion, and rejoice in the Lord your God: for he hath given you the former rain moderately, and he will cause to come down for you the rain, the former rain, and the latter rain in the first month. (Joel 2:12-13, 15, 18-19, 23)

In this passage, the inhabitants of Judah were once again facing trouble. They needed the anointing of deliverance, so they paid the price. They brought everyone together to fast and pray.

In response to their fast God gave them a promise—rain. As we have seen, rain is symbolic of the anointing (Zechariah 10:1). In promising rain, God was guaranteeing them the power to overcome the tribulation they were experiencing. They would be delivered by the power of the anointing. Not only would they be delivered, they would be blessed beyond their wildest dreams!

And the floors shall be full of wheat, and the vats shall overflow with wine and oil.

And I will restore to you the years that the locust hath eaten, the cankerworm, and the caterpiller, and the palmerworm, my great army which I sent among you.

And ye shall eat in plenty, and be satisfied, and praise the name of the Lord your God, that hath dealt wondrously with you: and my people shall never be ashamed.

And ye shall know that I am in the midst of Israel, and that I am the Lord your God, and none else: and my people shall never be ashamed.

And it shall come to pass afterward, that I will pour out my spirit upon all flesh; and your sons and daughters shall prophesy, your old men shall dream dreams, your young men shall see visions:

And also upon the servants and upon the handmaids in those days will I pour out my spirit.

And I will shew wonders in the heavens and in the earth, blood, and fire, and pillars of smoke. (Joel 2:24-30)

What did God say must be done in order to trigger such wondrous blessings? Seek Him through prayer and fasting. You, like the people of Judah, must give of yourself in exchange for an outpouring of victory from God.

Don't Mess with God's Anointed

In the book of Esther we find another beautiful example of God's people tapping into the delivering power of the anointing through fasting and prayer.

In this case, Mordecai, a righteous Jew, refused to dishonor God by bowing down to man. This caused great problems for the captive Jews, but once again we see the power to get results come on the scene as a result of fasting and prayer.

You are probably familiar with the story. Esther, a beautiful Jewish girl had been elevated to the position of Queen of Persia. Her uncle, Mordecai, had become the target of a plot by one of the king's aides, Haman, who conspired to kill him and all the Jews of the land.

When Esther and Mordecai learned of Haman's scheme, they declared a fast.

Then Esther bade them return to Mordecai this answer,

Go, gather together all the Jews that are present in Shushan, and fast ye for me, and neither eat nor drink three days, night or day: I also and my maidens will fast likewise; and so will I go in unto the king, which is not according to the law: and if I perish, I perish. (Esther 4:15-16)

Esther and her people paid the price for the power to get results. When she went to the king she found favor in his sight. (Remember, favor is one of the benefits of the anointing.) Not only were the Jews delivered, but the very gallows that had been intended for Mordecai were used to execute Haman!

So they hanged Haman on the gallows that he had prepared for Mordecai. (Esther 7:10)

When the anointing is present in your life, the evil things your enemies plan for you end up coming upon them instead.

The anointing also, as we saw in the life of Saul, brings with it a change of status.

And the king took off his ring, which he had taken from Haman, and gave it unto Mordecai. And Esther set Mordecai over the house of Haman. For Mordecai the Jew was next unto the king Ahasuerus, and great

among the Jews, and accepted of the multitude of his brethren, seeking the wealth of his people, and speaking peace to all his seed. (Esther 8:2, 10:3)

For Mordecai and Esther, promotion came as a result of the anointing. The anointing came because they were willing to pay the price. In fact, all of the Jews in captivity experienced a great victory in the time of Esther. When they called a fast and began to pray, the Spirit and the anointing of God came on them and they were able to produce results. They began to win. They began to move forward.

If there is any area in your life in which you need direction, make a quality decision to fast, pray and seek the Lord. When you do, you are guaranteed to receive the anointing and all of the benefits that come with it.

Are you willing to pay the price? Are you prepared to make an exchange? If so, you will be hooked into the power source that never runs dry. It is the anointing that brings you guaranteed victory. Hallelujah! Fasting and prayer will bring you the anointing.

Chapter 8
The Fruit of the Spirit
and the Anointing

"But the fruit of the Spirit is love, joy, peace, longsuffering, gentleness, goodness, faith, Meekness, temperance: against such there is no law." Galatians 5:22-23

Any time the topic of "the anointing" is discussed among believers, you will hear lots of talk about the "gifts" of the Spirit. Rarely, if ever, will you hear mention of the "fruit" of the Spirit. That is unfortunate, since there is a close correlation between the fruit of the Spirit and the anointing. They work together powerfully. When you understand how they relate, you can use them to win in every area of your life.

We have already established that the Holy Spirit is a "person", not an "it." He has a personality. That personality, just like anyone else's, produces an outward display of what is inside. We call that display His "character."

The concepts of character and personality are inseparably intertwined. As a matter of fact, when a person behaves in a way that is contrary to his personality, we say his behavior is "out of character." We say that because behavior or character is nearly always consistent with personality.

The same principle applies when discussing the Holy Spirit. Whenever you see the manifestation of the anointing, you should also see His character. What is His character like? You will find a description of it in **Galatians 5:22-23.**

> **But the fruit of the Spirit is love, joy, peace, long-suffering, gentleness, goodness, faith,**
>
> **Meekness, temperance: against such there is no law.**

Your Character Too!

Those nine characteristics, the fruit of the Spirit, are the very character of God. They are the character of Jesus. He was a walking manifestation of the fruit of the Spirit. In a very real sense, the fruit of the Spirit is the "image" of Christ.

In the light of that, read **Romans 8:29.**

For whom he did foreknow, he also did predestinate to be comformed to the image of his Son, that he might be the first-born among many brethren.

God has predestined us to be made into the *image* of Jesus! He has appointed us to bear the same spiritual fruit. In fact, the ultimate purpose of God's Word, the anointing, the Holy Ghost, the name of Jesus and the entire New Covenant is to transform us and make our character just like His.

"But, brother Dollar," you say, "I could never be like Jesus!"

Yes, you can! When you were born-again, the seed of His image was planted on the inside of you in your spirit-man. When you received the anointing of the Holy Ghost, His character was painted on you in power! What more could you need?

Powerful Fruit

The fruit of the Spirit is more than optional equipment in the Christian life. It is more than just a list of pleasant qualities every believer should try to possess. The fruit of the Spirit is a powerful component in the overcoming life, and is crucial to those who want to operate in the gifts of the Spirit.

When people try to operate in a gift of the Holy Spirit without the fruit of the Spirit, the gift becomes corrupted and does not operate in its fullness. Jesus gets no glory from such abuse of the anointing. (And remember, the primary purpose of the anointing is to glorify Him. See John 16:14.) Therefore, it is imperative that the power of the anointing be used in harmony with and under the powerful influence of the fruit of the Spirit.

If you want to see the true power of the fruit, look back at Galatians 5:23 and notice the last phrase: ". . .*against such there is no law.*" That literally means nothing can stand against these attributes. No force on earth is more powerful than these characteristics. These nine characteristics have the ability to get results. Nothing can stop them from producing what they are supposed to produce.

Why are they so potent? They are the personality traits of the Holy Spirit, and therefore, have His power behind them. The fruit of the Spirit is empowered by the anointing! The fruit of the Spirit always wins, because the power behind it is the source of "sweatless" victory.

Ask yourself, "Is my *joy* victorious over depression?," "Is *peace* defeating a tendency to worry?," "Is *faith* overcoming a spirit of fear?" If the answer is "no," you are not manifesting the Holy Ghost-empowered fruit of the Spirit. Genuine fruit of the Spirit has the power to get the job done.

Be Ultra-Fruitful

You may be wondering, *If the fruit of the Spirit is so powerful. . .and if it is already inside me. . .why doesn't it operate more fully in my life?* Good question! Remember we learned how operating in the anointing involves paying a price? Well, operating in the fruit of the Spirit also involves paying a price. Even though it is already on the inside of you, there is a price to pay if you want it fully manifested in your life.

Your spirit-man works much like your body. Every physiologically normal person, for instance, has a bicep muscle on each arm. Yet some people have large, powerful biceps, while others have small, weak ones. Genetic factors aside, the reason for this difference is exercise. Some people work their muscles more than others. They apply pressure in order to develop the muscle. The same principle applies to the fruit of the Spirit.

As you grow and mature as a Christian, the fruit naturally grows and develops. It is a natural part of the process. However, if you apply the necessary pressure, the growth will be more dramatic and pronounced. You will become ultra-fruitful.

Cultivating Your Harvest

Why do some Christians develop this ultra-fruitfulness and others do not? Look back at the scripture we read in **Isaiah 55:1** and you will see.

Ho, every one that thirsteth, come ye to the waters, and he that hath no money; come ye, buy, and eat; yea, come, buy wine and milk without money and without price.

The reason some believers never exhibit any growth or development of the fruit of the Spirit is they have not been hungry and thirsty enough to cultivate it.

In the natural, you can tell the difference between a farmer who *really* wants a harvest and one who does not, by the amount of time and effort each one spends in cultivation. The farmer who wants a bountiful harvest will work very hard and consistently to take care of his crop. The other will do just enough to get by.

You see that in the spiritual realm as well. Those who are *really* hungry to exhibit the characteristics of the Holy Ghost will spend more time working and cultivating in order to develop them. It all depends on how badly you want them.

Isaiah said those that were thirsty needed to go to the waters and buy. Something must be given out before anything can be received. Unfortunately some people have developed a "welfare mentality" about the fruit of the Spirit. They want a handout. They want to stand in a prayer line and have the minister lay hands on them to receive more faith. It does not come that way.

If you want bigger faith, you will have to grow and cultivate the little faith you already possess. Soon it will begin to mature and flourish. If you find that your "joy" only works a little bit, you have probably only cultivated it a little bit.

Faith and joy are only two of the characteristics or "fruit" of the Spirit, but they are all developed in the same way. You "buy" them with diligence, practice and effort. Once they are yours, they will never, ever fail.

Developing the fruit of the Spirit is not an event, it is a process which requires work. Many people see strong brothers and sisters in Christ and want to immediately have the love, joy or peace that they possess. What they fail to appreciate is all the practice that was required to develop those attributes. They do not see all the times that person had to bite their tongue when an unkind word tried to leave their lips. They do not see the perseverance in tribulation that brought them to where they are now. All they see is the end result.

If you really want the fruit of the Spirit, get started on the cultivation process today! Make a quality decision to do whatever is necessary to make it grow. If you really want the power, come to the waters and buy.

Chapter 9
The Fruit of Temperance
and the Anointing

"And every man that striveth for the mastery is temperate in all things." I Corinthians 9:25

The fruit of the Spirit plays an indispensable role in bringing you victory in life. Each one is an awesomely powerful weapon in the arsenal of the anointing. Yet one stands out from all the others in importance in helping you operate in the power of God—that is *temperance*.

I can hear some of you now, "Temperance? You've got to be kidding? I'm not even sure I know what it is!"

Well, it is time you found out, because without it, you can forget about tapping into the full power of the anointing.

Who's the Boss?

Temperance basically means "self-control." It is the ability to control the flesh and bring it into subjection to the spirit. When you develop temperance, your flesh and soul no longer dictate your course of action.

If you fail to develop temperance, you will never be in a position to give an appropriate exchange for the anointing. A lack of will-power and self-discipline will characterize your entire spiritual life. When you want to get up early and pray, you will not because your flesh will say you are too tired. When you want to fast and seek the face of God, you will not because your flesh will demand otherwise. Without temperance, what the flesh wants, the flesh gets.

Once your flesh starts calling the shots, your mind will be more than willing to jump on the bandwagon and provide great rationalizations. It will tell you, "You don't have to go to all that trouble to have the anointing. After all, it's already on the inside of you! Forget about disciplining your flesh. You can just call on the anointing if you get into trouble."

Your mind and body will convince you that there is no need to fast and pray. Then one day when trouble arrives, you will discover that your spiritual power has been turned off because you have not been paying the bill.

There are no two ways about it. If you want to operate in the anointing as God desires you to, you are going to have to develop the fruit of temperance. Paul said it well:

Know ye not that they which run in a race run all, but one receiveth the prize? So run, that ye may obtain. And every man that striveth for the mastery is temperate in all things. Now they do it to obtain a corruptible crown; but we an incorruptible.

I therefore so run, not as uncertainly; so fight I, not as one that beateth the air: But I keep under my body, and bring it into subjection: lest that by any means when I have preached to others, I myself should be a castaway. (I Corinthians 9:24-27)

Paul warns that unless you get your body under control, you will become a castaway. In the Greek, the word translated castaway means unapproved, rejected, worthless and reprobate (void of judgement). That is a pretty stiff warning! Yet he does not stop there. He continues with the word, "Moreover." *Moreover* means that what follows is even more important than what preceded. So, let's take a close look at what Paul says next.

Overthrown in the Wilderness.
Moreover, brethren, I would not that ye should be ignorant, how that all our fathers were under the cloud, and all passed through the sea; And were all

baptized unto Moses in the cloud and in the sea; And did all eat the same spiritual meat; And did all drink the same spiritual drink: for they drank of that spiritual Rock that followed them: and that Rock was Christ. But with many of them God was not well pleased: for they were overthrown in the wilderness.

Now these things were for examples, to the intent we should not lust after evil things, as they also lusted. Neither be ye idolaters, as were some of them; as it is written, The people sat down to eat and drink, and rose up to play. Neither let us commit fornication, as some of them committed, and fell in one day three and twenty thousand. Neither let us tempt Christ as some of them also tempted and were destroyed of serpents. Neither murmur ye, as some of them also murmured, and were destroyed of the destroyer.

There hath no temptation taken you but such as is common to man: but God is faithful, who will not suffer you to be tempted above that ye are able; but will with the temptation also make a way to escape, that ye may be able to bear it. (I Corinthians 10:1-10, 13)

The Israelites fell and were overthrown (the Greek word translated *overthrown* means slain or killed) because of a problem they had in the wilderness. What was that problem? A lack of temperance.

To show you how that same problem affects us today, let's read the first five verses of that passage again, translating the Old Covenant imagery into New Covenant reality.

v.1) ...*our fathers were under the cloud*... "Joe Christian was under the covering of God and had been delivered from the bondage of his pre-salvation life."

v.2) ...*and all passed through the sea and were baptized unto Moses in the cloud and in the sea*... "And he was baptized in the Holy Ghost with the evidence of speaking in tongues and had the anointing inside of him."

v.3)   ...*And all did eat the same spiritual meat*... "And he ate spiritual teaching from Kenneth Copeland, Kenneth Hagin and the entire TBN family."

v.4)   ...*And did all drink the same spiritual drink: for they drank of that spiritual Rock that followed them, and that Rock was Christ*... "He even drank from the well of eternal life."

v.5)   ...*But with many of them God was not well pleased: for they were overthrown in the wilderness*... "But God could not give him the power to get results in its fullness because every time pressure came to his flesh he was defeated due to a lack of temperance or self-control."

Child of God, that which happened to Israel in the wilderness can also happen to you. You may have wonderful blessings from God, but you will never see the promised land of "sweatless victory in the anointing" if you lose control of your flesh and sin every time the pressure hits. You must master your flesh. You must develop temperance.

The Fatal Four

There were four major areas in which the children of Israel were overcome: idolatry, fornication, tempting Christ and murmuring. Keeping in mind that each one of these can be overcome with temperance, let's examine these "fatal four" more closely.

Idolatry

Thou shalt not make unto thee any graven image, or any likeness of any thing that is in heaven above, or that is in the earth beneath, or that is in the water under earth: Thou shalt not bow down thyself to them, nor serve them: for I the Lord thy God am a jealous God, visiting the iniquity of the fathers upon the children unto the third and fourth generation of them that hate me. (Exodus 20:4-5)

Obviously, very few believers today are battling an urge to make an image of a cow and bow down before it. However, possession of a graven image is not necessary in order to be involved in idolatry. As Paul indicates in Colossians 3:5, idolatry takes many forms.

Mortify therefore your members which are upon the earth; fornication, uncleanness, inordinate affection, evil concupiscence, and covetousness, which is idolatry.

Many Christians are involved in idolatry in the sense that they are serving or giving a disproportionate amount of their affection to things other than God. For example, I used to have a weakness for apple pie. Apple pie was very, very good *to* me, but it was not very good *for* me. Praise God, through the fruit of temperance I now have that appetite under control.

Whatever you work for, whatever enslaves you or keeps you in bondage is your idol. It could be cigarettes, money, slothfulness, pride, your job, television or even your spouse. If it comes before obeying the Word, then it is your idol.

Fornication

The second member of the "Fatal Four", fornication, in its most literal form involves sex between two people outside of the confines of marriage. I hope I do not have to tell you, it is wrong!

Before you start congratulating yourself for being free from fornication, however, let me tell you something. Although illicit sex is the most obvious and blatant form of fornication, there is a more subtle form. It is a form that many people are involved in without even realizing it! I am talking about spiritual fornication, which has the same deadly effects as its physical counterpart.

What is spiritual fornication? In the eyes of God it is simply close friendship with the things of the world.

Ye adulterers and adulteresses, know ye not that the friendship of the world is enmity with God? Whosoever therefore will be a friend of the world is the enemy of God. (James 4:4)

The world's system and way of operation is diametrically opposed to God. Therefore, when you line yourself up with the world's system, you involve yourself with something in opposition to your bridegroom, Jesus Christ. That is spiritual fornication.

You can either operate your finances according to the world's system or the Word's system. The choice is yours. You can live life the world's way or God's way. The way you choose is determined by the focus of your love.

Love not the world, neither the things that are in the world. If any man love the world, the love of the Father is not in him. For all that is in the world, the lust of the flesh, and the lust of the eyes, and the pride of life, is not of the Father, but is of the world. And the world passeth away, and the lust thereof: but he that doeth the will of God abideth for ever. (I John 2:15-17)

When temperance is operating in your life, you have the power to choose God's way of doing things. Temperance protects you from falling into both types of fornication, physical and spiritual.

Tempting Christ

Another function of the fruit of temperance is to prevent you from "tempting Christ." To "tempt Christ" is to speak against God's rightfully ordained authority. You can see an example of such behavior in **Numbers 21:5-6:**

And the people spake against God, and against Moses, Wherefore have ye brought us up out of Egypt to die in the wilderness? for there is no bread, neither is there any water; and our soul loatheth this light

bread. And the Lord sent fiery serpents among the people, and they bit the people; and much people of Israel died.

By speaking against God and against His designated leader, Moses, the children of Israel tempted God. When they did, they died.

Obviously, God takes this sort of thing very seriously— not just in the Old Testament but in the New Testament as well. In **Galatians 5:19-21**, Paul calls it *sedition*.

Now the works of the flesh are manifest, which are these: Adultery, fornication, uncleanness, lasciviousness, idolatry, witchcraft . . . ,seditions, . . . murders . . . they which do such things shall not inherit the kingdom of God.

Sedition is an incitement of resistance against lawful authority, and is listed by Paul among uncleanness, witchcraft and murder. So do not fool yourself into thinking it is no big deal. God hates it!

Child of God, please do not tempt Christ by speaking against His anointed. Speak only the Word and that which is positive—especially where it concerns those who are in spiritual authority over you. Do not speak against your pastor. If you are having problems submitting to your pastor or spiritual leadership in any other form, keep your mouth shut, pray over the situation and exercise the fruit of temperance. Trust me, it is in your best interest to do so. (See Hebrews 13:17.)

Murmuring

The final member of the "Fatal Four" that temperance helps you overcome is murmuring. Murmuring is complaining about circumstances and situations that apply uncomfortable pressure to your flesh.

I Corinthians 10:10 says, **Neither murmur ye, as some of them also murmured, and were destroyed of the destroyer.**

It is easy to fall into murmuring while in the middle of assigned tasks. Don't do it. Murmuring will not make them any easier; in fact, it will make them more difficult. When you are tempted to complain, exercise temperance and force your mouth, mind and flesh to line up with the Word of God. Then, do all that you do in a spirit of joy as unto the Lord.

How to Cultivate the Fruit of Temperance

Although temperance is a powerful force that can unleash the anointing in many areas of your life, it does not come easily. It requires MUCH cultivation. So do not give it a half-hearted try and then give up in discouragement. Roll up your spiritual sleeves, get determined and get busy doing the following three things.

1. Tame that Tongue.

The first thing you must do in order to develop the fruit of temperance is learn how to control your mouth.

I remember one point early in my marriage when my wife and I were having a "discussion." She told me to stop yelling at her. "I'M NOT YELLING!!!" I heard myself scream. When I realized what I was doing, I knew I needed help. I went into the next room and prayed, "Lord, help me. I need temperance. I need some self-control."

Taming your tongue will give you temperance. **James 3:1-6** tells us why this is so important.

My brethren, be not many masters, knowing that we shall receive the greater condemnation. For in many things we offend all. If any man offend not in word, the same is a perfect man, and able also to bridle the whole body. Behold, we put bits in the horses mouths, that they may obey us; and we turn about their whole body. Behold also the ships, which though they be so great, and are driven of fierce

winds, yet are they turned about with a very small helm, withersoever the governor listeth. Even so the tongue is a little member, and boasteth great things.

Behold, how great a matter a little fire kindleth! And the tongue is a fire, a world of iniquity: so is the tongue among our members, that it defileth the whole body, and setteth on fire the course of nature; and it is set on fire of hell.

Words are important. Words got you your house. Words got you your car. Words got you your name. Words describe who you are. Words! Words! Words! This is a word created world we are living in, and, as this passage of scripture points out, there is a relationship between your body and the words that come out of your mouth.

Your tongue can defile your whole body. The words that come out of your mouth will determine what will be in your flesh. If you have words of sickness and poverty in your mouth, your body will be turned and will begin to flow in that direction just as surely as a bit in a horse's mouth turns the horse. On the other hand, if you continually speak words of health and prosperity, that is where you will end up. It is up to you!

Words are potent. They created the entire universe (Hebrews 11:3). They can also create temperance in your life. If you will diligently speak words of life, strength, discipline and victory, you will begin to gain mastery over your flesh. If you speak words of slothfulness, laziness and gluttony, that is precisely the direction in which your flesh will head. You must control your mouth or your mouth will control you.

2. Build Up Your Spirit-Man.

"The spirit indeed is willing, but the flesh is weak." That's what Jesus said about his disciples in Matthew 26:41. He had specifically asked them to pray for Him while He went through His temptation in the Garden of Gethsemane. When He returned from praying, He found them asleep.

Sadly, at that time in their lives, the disciples' spirits had no control over their flesh.

A lot of Christians today have the same problem. If you are one of them, I have good news for you. You need not live a willing-spirit-weak-flesh life! You have the ability to build up your spirit-man, and make it strong enough to overcome even the weakest areas of your flesh. How? Look at **Galatians 5:16.**

This I say then, Walk in the Spirit, and ye shall not fulfill the lust of the flesh.

The way to have victory over the lusts of the flesh is to walk in the Spirit. We do that by simply walking in line with the Word. Jesus said His words are spirit and life (John 6:63). If you want to walk according to the Spirit, walk by the Word. When you do, you will build up your spirit man.

Another way to develop the inner man is through speaking in tongues. Tongues is designed to build you up.

But ye, beloved, building up yourselves on your most holy faith, praying in the Holy Ghost. (Jude 20.)

He that speaketh in an unknown tongue edifieth (builds up) himself. . . (I Corinthians 14:4)

Tongues can and will build you up spiritually. With a strong spirit-man, you can overcome the weakness of the flesh.

3. Amazing Grace

The last powerful way to develop temperance is by getting an understanding of and receiving God's grace.

Grace is simply undeserved love and favor. You and I do not deserve to enjoy the wonderful promises of God, but we receive them anyway because of His grace. We did not do anything to earn them, Jesus did it for us. Believers who do not understand grace give up and quit once they have been overcome by their flesh a couple of times. They fail to develop temperance because they think they must do it on their own. However, **Hebrews 4:16** says:

Let us therefore come boldly unto the throne of grace, that we may obtain mercy, and find grace to help in time of need.

When your flesh tries to control your life, go boldly to the throne of grace. Don't go through all that "I'm not worthy" garbage! Just receive God's grace. It is there to help you. It is there to provide access to God so that you can draw near to Him in your darkest hour. It is there so that you can come to His throne without hesitation or reservation and say, "Lord, help me," and He will be there.

Once you recognize your position in grace, you will begin to have temperance and self-control. Why? Because you will be bold enough to go to God in a time of need to ask for help in developing it.

When you mess up, you will not quit. You will get up and get back in the battle. As you do, God's grace will help you continue until you have gained mastery over your flesh. God's grace will bring you closer than ever to experiencing the fullness of the anointing.

Chapter 10
Love and the Anointing:
Keeping His Word

"Love never fails."
I Corinthians 13:8 (NASB)

We have already seen the strong relationship between the fruit of the Spirit and the anointing. Both, working separately and together, give us the ability to win. We have also seen that no law or force can stand against the fruit of the Spirit.

No trouble, tribulation or circumstance can overcome you if these forces are prevalent in your life. Once you have cultivated them, no hate, depression, insecurity, wavering, violence, evil, doubt, pride or lasciviousness will prevail against you.

The fruit of the Spirit guarantees victory. The evidence of their power may not be instantaneous, but once you have paid the price, you will not lose.

The Greatest of These. . .

Nothing in God's Word is placed there randomly or haphazardly. So it is important to note the order in which the fruit of the Spirit are listed in **Galatians 5:22-23: love, joy, peace, longsuffering, gentleness, goodness, faith, Meekness, temperance.** God has listed these forces in this order to indicate their rank and importance in our lives.

The first one on the list is "love." Love is the most important and powerful force of all. Without it, joy will not work. Without joy, peace will not work. Without peace, longsuffering will not work. Without longsuffering, gentleness will not work. Without gentleness, goodness will not work. Without goodness, faith will not work. Without faith, meekness will not work. And without meekness, temperance will not work. That is their order.

Notice that without the fruit of love, none of them will work. Love is the most important thing. It is the key to operating in all the rest of the fruit of the Spirit.

That is essentially what Paul was saying in I Corinthians 13:13.

But now abideth faith, hope, love, these three; but the greatest of these is love. (NASB)

Now, you know that faith is an awesomely powerful force. And hope, according to Hebrews 6:19, is the very anchor of the soul. Yet, according to Paul, love is bigger and more important than both of them.

Love = Non-Stop Victory

Like the anointing, love gives you the ability to win against all odds. It literally never fails. Why? Because God never fails and "God is Love" (I John 4:8). Love is consistent and diligent in accomplishing what you need accomplished in your life. It will not stop working until it has given you victory. Love even works to energize your faith. **Galatians 5:6** says that **"faith worketh by love."** Since love never fails, when you speak to the mountains in your life with faith in your heart (Mark 11:23-24), and that faith is powered by the force of love, those mountains must move. Love makes your faith unstoppable.

That is easy to understand when you consider the fact that the biggest hindrance to your faith is fear. As we learn from **I John 4:18, "There is no fear in love; but perfect love casteth out fear. . ."** If you will cultivate the fruit of love in your life, those faith-stopping fears that have held you back for so long will be cast out forever! Love will give you victory.

Keeping His Word

John 14:15 says, "If ye love me, keep my commandments."

Here, Jesus very plainly tells us that we demonstrate real love for Him when we obey Him. Therefore, one of the best ways to show your love for God is by doing His Word.

But whoso keepeth his word, in him verily is the love of God perfected: hereby know we that we are in him. (I John 2:5)

When you combine these two truths: (1) Perfect love casts out all fear and (2) the love of God is perfected in us when we *keep His Word:* you find that "doing" God's Word is the key to developing the love that casts out fear. When we "do" the word, our love is made perfect. When our love is made perfect, then our joy, peace, longsuffering, etc. can also be made perfect. Then we can truly say that we will never fail.

Love is a force that cannot be stopped. Yet, keeping the Word is only one side of the coin of love. The flip side involves developing an intimate love relationship with God. Read on and you will find out how.

Chapter 11
Love and the Anointing:
Developing a Love Relationship with the Father

"Thou shalt love the Lord thy God with all thy heart, and with all thy soul, and with all thy mind. This is the first and great commandment." **Matthew 22:37-38**

Thus far, we have seen how humility, prayer, fasting and the fruit of the Spirit all play a part in positioning the believer to receive the power to get results. All of these are vitally important elements in an anointed believer's life. Yet there is one other. This element is more important (and more rewarding) than any of the others discussed thus far.

I am talking about paying the price for the anointing through loving fellowship with the Father. It is a price too many are not willing to pay. Too many people want the power without the personal relationship. They are interested in receiving God's miracles, healings and benefits, but they do not care to know Him as a person.

In a way, these people want to "take advantage" of God. They want the benefits of marriage without the commitment. They want to have the expensive outfit from the department store without paying the price for it. Sadly, people who think this way will get nowhere.

Even many preachers and teachers pray, fast and read the Word only in an attempt to get God's power. They have the right actions, but their motivation is wrong. It is good and proper to use fasting and prayer as an exchange for the anointing—but only when your ultimate heart motivation is to grow in intimacy with God.

Closer Than a Brother

How well do you know the know the Holy Spirit? Do you treat Him well? Do you greet Him? When you wake up in the morning, what do you say to Him?

Every morning when I get up, I walk out of my room towards my prayer room at the end of the hall. I have my blanket on my shoulder. I look like Linus from "Peanuts." When I get to the end of the hallway, I enter into the room and close the door. I say, "Good morning, Holy Spirit." Do you know what I hear Him say? He says, "Good morning. How are you? Are you ready for today?"

I reply, "Yes." Then I begin to pray.

After I have finished praying, there is silence. I want to give the Holy Spirit time to talk to me. Prayer should never be a monologue, it should be a dialogue. I begin to talk to Him and He talks to me. He warns me of things. He shows me things. He shows me what I need for the day and what I need to be careful of. He asks me to judge myself in different areas of my life. I do, so I can be closer to Him.

Then, I begin to pray in the spirit and dig deep inside of me. I pour out all that I have inside of me before the Father. I empty myself before Him so that He can fill me with His love and His presence.

As I walk out of the room, I praise and worship Him. The Holy Spirit is not imaginary. He is more real than real itself. He is a person. When I am driving my car, I open my mouth and talk to Him. I am not concerned about what people say when they look at me thinking that I am crazy, because I know that I have an invisible friend who is there with me. I know that He is there with me, therefore, I do not ignore Him, and act like He is not. I welcome Him and the host of angels that come with Him.

In the midst of my counseling sessions and all throughout the day, I say, "Father, give me wisdom. Give me wisdom, Lord." And He always does!

And at the end of the day, I say, "Lord, my body is tired, but I thank you that your strength goes from everlasting to everlasting. I love you, Lord." I hear Him say, "I love you too, son." When I hear "son", I know it is the Father talking to me.

In any temptation that I have there is not much pressure because I do not want to disappoint He who watches as I sleep, who wakes me up and who fellowships with me every moment of the day. I think of Him through the night. I never have nightmares. My dreams are not dreams of defeat but of victory. I dream about His Word overcoming the enemy.

The Word that I meditate on before I lay my head on the pillow is the same Word that wakes me up in the morning. I am filled with His presence. In the time of trouble, I can go to Him as a friend, a friend with whom I have diligently worked everyday to develop an intimate relationship. When I go to Him, He is always there. He is my friend that sticketh closer than a brother.

Now ask yourself, "Do I have that kind of relationship?" If you do not, then you must begin to work on developing one. It is impossible to know or experience the personality of the Holy Spirit any other way.

Your First Priority

Nothing takes precedence over knowing and loving God. In Matthew 22, Jesus said:

Thou shalt love the Lord thy God with all thy heart, and with all thy soul, and with all thy mind. This is the first and great commandment. (verses 37-38)

We are commanded to love God more than anyone or anything. Most "religious" folks would claim that this is a very easy thing to do. I disagree. When I first got saved,

I had a difficult time loving God more than anyone—especially my mother. I could not honestly say that I loved God more than her. The truth was that I loved my mother more than I loved God. And for a very good reason—I knew her better!

No one can ever truthfully say they love someone until they have spent time with that person. When I was first saved, I had not spent any real time with God. Therefore, it was impossible for me to say I truly loved Him. Now, however, I can say that I love him more than anything else in this world with great confidence because I have spent quality time growing in love with him. It was a gradual process that involved hours and hours, days and days, and years and years of work and sacrifice. My love for Him still grows, and it will continue to do so throughout eternity.

God wants to know you and fellowship with you personally. He wants you to know Him intimately so He can clothe you with His power and ability. The more "personal" your relationship with the Father becomes, the more you will be able to operate in His "personality."

Knowing and loving your Heavenly Father is the most important matter in your life. **Matthew 7:22-23** dramatically illustrates this fact.

Many will say to me in that day, Lord, Lord, have we not prophesied in thy name? and in thy name cast out devils? and in thy name done many wonderful works? And then will I profess unto them, I never knew you: depart from me, ye that work iniquity.

As we see in this verse, many people mistakenly believe that they can express their love to the Father solely through their good works. That certainly is one way to show God you love him, but unless you *know* Him, you will not be able to stay with Him in eternity.

The word "knew" in verse 23 means to know by experience or effort. It implies knowledge gained as a result of prolonged practice. That kind of "knowing" requires intimacy. The Bible says in Genesis 4:1 that Adam "knew" Eve. This does not mean that Adam got acquainted with her. It means that he was physically intimate with her. He became one with her. That is how God wants to know you—intimately.

Such "knowing" will cost you. It requires time and effort. It means you will have to give up your plans and your will in order to discover His plans and His will.

Know Him First in the Word

Practically speaking, there are two major things you can do to cultivate a love relationship with your Heavenly Father. The first one is this: Search His Word.

You need to discover what God is like. So look in the Word to find out about Him. Use it to explore His ways and His manner of doing things. Jesus said, "If you've seen me, you've seen the Father" (John 14:9). Therefore, you can look at the life and character of Jesus in the Bible and find out about God.

You can find out why God does what He does and why He reacts to certain behaviors in certain ways. If you will search Him out, He will reveal Himself to you. Remember, God rewards those who diligently seek Him (Hebrews 11:6). As He does, your senses will become attuned to Him. You will begin to find that you know what is *of* Him and what is not. Then you can move to the next step toward developing an intimate relationship with Him.

Spend quality time with God

This is supremely important. You must spend quiet, quality time alone with your Heavenly Father. Doing so may require a great sacrifice on your part. You may have to discipline your flesh and get up before the rest of the house is stirring. You may have to give up television and movies. You will probably even need to give up some fellowship time with your brothers and sisters in Christ!

I know from experience that even seemingly spiritual activities can begin to rob you of the indispensable time with God. Early in my ministry, I would spend great amounts of time in my room fasting and praying. I would lay aside every distraction and commune with God. As a result, I had His anointing. I had His plan.

Shortly thereafter, I discovered what caused great ministries to fall. In many cases it was not pride or sin, it was the distractions, the demands of schedules and people. People can become so busy—going here to preach, going there to counsel, attending this meeting, attending that conference—that they completely schedule out the beautiful fellowship time with the Holy Spirit.

I saw myself falling into the very same trap! All of the people, all of the departments and all of the problems had become a distraction. Although I was still getting up early to spend time with the Lord, He had become just another item on my schedule. There was no flexibility for the Holy Spirit to say, "Can we talk?" If He did, I would have had to respond, "No Lord, I have a counseling session."

When I came to that realization, the Lord cautioned me. He said, "Choose."

We all have to make that choice. You will choose whether to make time with God your top priority or to let your life-giving anointing be ruined by the demands of people and schedules.

Making all else secondary to time with God may sound drastic, but it is nothing in comparison to the joys and rewards of intimacy with the Father. For those who are truly thirsty for God's power, the choice is a simple one.

The Anointing is for You

The awesome endowment of heaven's power is not just for prominent television preachers. It is not reserved only for specially selected men and women of God. It is God's fervent desire that you operate in the anointing too! He has made it available for you.

He wants to clothe you with His power and ability. It is His ability that will give you the power to get results in every endeavor. He wants to bring glory to His name by empowering you to walk in "sweatless" victory over the enemy.

The crucial questions for you at this moment are, "How badly do you want the anointing?" and "How much are you willing to give to walk in the anointing?".

I trust your answer is, "Whatever it takes!"